What leading Authors & Clergy-members have to say:

I am absolutely astounded to find a non-Christian produce such a work.
- *Rev. Reginald Corfield, Methodist Church, NJ*

I sense in the Author, the Spirit of Christ, that I love and serve.
- *Rev. Dr. Donald H. Hillyard, The Church in the Garden, NY*

I commend you for your knowledge and understanding of Christianity.
- *Rev. Dr. Dale T. Irvin, Pastor, NY Theological Seminary, NY*

Impressed by your Faith in Prayer for Godly-Union.
- *Rev. Msgr. T.D. Candreva, St. Raymond-of-Penyafort, NY*

…a remarkable manifestation of Spiritual Power in all aspects of life.
- *Rev. Msgr. James E. Boesel, Our Lady Of Mercy, NY*

Commendable endeavor toward building bridges across religious boundaries.
- *Dr. Gurcharan Singh, Prof.-Emeritus Intl.-Studies Mary Mount Coll., NY*

…the TRUE One's Truthful-Gift, through Author, to humanity.
- *Singh Sahib J. S. Jaachak, Former Head-Priest Golden Temple, India*

The Author has demonstrated why people need the Lord, and who God is.
- *Rev. Reginald Nuameh, Episcopal Church, Brooklyn, NY*

A wonderful comparative study… an exciting and excellent reading.
Singh Sahib Jiwan Singh Khalsa, Regional Director, Sikh Dharma, NY

This is a very resourceful & educative, and highly spiritual piece of work.
- *Rev. Gbenga Famojuro, Christ Apostolic Church, Brooklyn, NY*

It is really a wonderful book, which touched my heart deeply.
- *Rev. Jacky Simte, Ph.D , Registrar Nazareth Bible College, Manipur*

Nice effort to present the belief-systems of both religions.
- *Revs. Mrs. & Mr. Costello,N. Shore Assembly of God, NY*

D1611913

This Book has been published under the aegis of :

DIVINE POWER, Inc.
(a/k/a ISHWAR FOUNDATION)
A Non-Profit-Organization

P.O. Box 226, Glen Cove, N.Y.11542.

www.divinepower.org   *info@divinepower.org*

Tel.: 516-676-7000   *Facsimile: 516-609-0704*

All esteemed readers are invited to participate in God's work, by donating any amount to the Non-Profit-Org.: DIVINE POWER, Inc., which is constantly striving for spreading the light of spirituality.

Donations are tax-deductible.

DEDICATION

I am highly honored
to dedicate this work to
the cherished and loving memory
of my dear father,
Mr. Kartar Singh Sabharwal,
_(1915-2000)_
*

My humble tributes to the man who
was, is, and shall remain my **Guide**
as if he was holding my pen
and dictating me the words,
just as he had held my hand as **Father**
helping me walk my first little steps,
taught me as a **Teacher**,
laughed with me as a **Friend**,
and led me by example as my **Mentor.**
His unflinching faith in the Creator
was manifest in his practice.
He devoted most of his life to the quest
of knowledge and selfless-service.
*

Bhappa ji and Bhabhi ji
We all miss you both
Your indebted family

Sdn. Nand Kaur & S. Harbhajan Singh
Sdn. Jasbir Kaur & S. Joginder Singh
Dr. Pritpal Singh & Sdn. Jasbir Kaur
Dr. Harsimran Singh & Dr. Satnam Kaur
S. Surinder Singh & Sdn. Jasleen Kaur
Dr. Amarjit Singh & Dr. Chanchal Kaur

FOREWORD

There is the famous saying : "Every mother considers her child the most beautiful and talented, wise and knowledgeable". Similarly, one would rightfully claim that theirs is the best religion ! It requires courage, which Dr. Harsimran Singh has plenty of, to dwell into to compare his own Sikh religion, with the dominant religion of the world, Christianity. Those who know the history and bravery of Sikh people, clearly understand the determination and courageous work of Dr. Singh. As an engineer, he is methodical and organized; as an entrepreneur, he is breaking new ground, and creating different paths.

Unlike turn of the century Sikh migrants into North America, who were relegated to menial and farming work, this new wave of highly educated and extremely smart Sikhs, who landed here in the sixties and seventies, have a lot to offer, to the multi-religious, multi-racial America. While earlier Sikhs, with their hard work, made gold out of farming, new immigrants are taking modern challenges and scaling even greater heights.

Dr. Singh's first book, <u>THE DIVINE TRUTH</u>, provides answers to modern-age torments; In his new book, <u>THE SPIRITUAL POWER</u>: A Gift of Christianity & Sikhism, he works tirelessly, to show common grounds. At present, he has done justice to his Faith, as well as to Christianity. I hope that he would endevor to work on other Faiths.

Arvind Vora, Chairman, Long Island Multi-Faith Forum, NY.

The Forum is represented by the following Religions/Faiths

Members:	representing
Ghazi Khankan and Sanaa Nadim	Al-Islam
Stacy Fagan and Bernice Suplee	Bahai'
Kala Iyengar and Erik Larson	Brahma Kumaris
Madeline Ko-I Bastis and Tenshin C. Gilhooly	Buddhism
Donald Beckman and Ann Mallouk	Christianity
Lance Bark and Chandni Duni	Hinduism
Mahendra Shah and Panna Shah	Jainism
Werner Reich and Bobbie Rozenzweig	Judaism
Samuel Beeler and Frank Schaefer	Native American Indian
Rajinderjit K. Singh and Sangat Singh Syalee	Sikhism

Preface
PRAYER : 'An inspirational Power'.

I am immensely grateful to the Divine Power, for bestowing His Grace on me, by manifesting His miraculous powers, in response to Prayers, thereby enhancing my faith, to accomplish almost impossible tasks.

Several wondrous miracles prodded me to write my first book, THE DIVINE TRUTH, based on spiritual quotations from the Holy Scripture of Sikhism, Sri Guru Granth Sahib, for the benefit of humanity at large.

This followed the encouragement that came in the form of a spate of observations from readers, especially Christians, that I should write a similar book based on Spirituality in Christianity. I wanted to offer my humble service, by writing the book, and I started exploring the means.

To my amazement, I could not find a single reference book based on Spirituality in Christianity, although there are innumerable books on religious and historical aspects. I surrenedered myself to the will of God and prayed to Him to help me. I was then reminded of the noble soul, Mother Teresa, who said: "We are, all, pens in the hands of God." In a similar vein, eminent Sikh scholar Dr. Bhai Vir Singhji had said: "As the body is rejuvenated by the flow of blood, so is the soul by the ink flowing from a blessed pen". This reassured me that God shall provide the requisite strength to my pen, for I mean to do good for humanity and fulfill a gap that has existed for centuries.

THE SPIRITUAL POWER is a comparative study of Christianity and Sikhism. To realize the distinctiveness of one, it is imperative that a comparison with another be made. To know the attraction of one color, another color must be at hand to truly appreciate similarities and differences.

Knowledge is of no avail, if not guided by wisdom, which ought to be derived from Holy Books. I've tried to take extracts from such texts, without prejudice to either, and in the simplest form, so as to serve as a daily guide for lay persons and students of comparative religions.

I shall try to touch the other Faiths, as and when commanded to do so. I've attempted to restrict myself to 'one page per topic', because my intention is neither to present a voluminous treatise that gathers dust on the shelf, nor to impress readers with any knowledge, of which I have none.

Dr. Harsimran Singh

Acknowledgments

"God works through His creations to accomplish His missions".

I acknowledge, with grateful thanks, the help provided by Rev. Gary Smith and his wife, Mrs. Brenda Smith. After having finalized the book, I laid my pen to rest; but my brain was as restless as ever, because I was anxious that I must do justice to all sects of Christianity. And, so I prayed for help. As it has happened on various occasions in my life, timely help arrived, in the form of a phone-call from Rev. Smith, who wanted my association in a community-project in Mastic, N.Y. He and his wife offered their help in reviewing the book. I seemed to "recognize" his voice, as if I had known him for years. When I went to meet them, Rev. Smith told me that he had dreamt that a "bearded and turbaned man" would shortly be visiting his Church.

I'm extremely thankful for the guidance provided by Rev. John Cherian, M.Th., D.D., Editor of Christian Anthropology publication, and Host of a television program, 'Precious Moments'. He is the former Dean of South Asia Bible College, Bangalore, India, and the former Pastor of Calvary United Methodist Church, Queens Village, New York. I'm grateful to the numerous Christian Scholars and Clergy-Members, for the time they took in reviewing the manuscript, as also for their gracious comments, from which one-line-extracts have been reproduced, on the cover (outside and inside); the learned academics may, or may not, be in full agreement with the entire text.

I acknowledge, with immense thanks, the information received from Ms. Anne Hastings of Mattel Interactive who permitted us to use their Bible Quick Verse Program.

I wish to go on record, by expressing my gratefulness, for unparalleled services, to Mr. Glenn Scott Bradley, for his timely help at all times. This humble Christian has been instrumental in establishing initial contact with several Christian Pastors and scholars.

I must acknowledge, with immense gratitude, some really tireless and commendable work done by my research-associate, Mr. Amarjit Singh Anand, who put his 'heart & soul' into the commissioned-research, for this project. His Spiritual-Orientation, coupled with an avid interest in the study of Comparative Religions became instrumental in our association.

I'm indebted to Singh Sahib Giani Jagtaar Singhji 'Jaachak', Head-Priest at Gurdwara-Sahib, Glen Cove, NY, for his esteemed guidance. He is the Former Head-Priest of The Golden-Temple (the Sanctum-Sanctorum of the Sikhs) in SriAmritsar, India.

My special thanks are due to S. Harpreet Singh, and S. Kuldip Singh, for their zealous effort in painstakingly reviewing the manuscript, especially the section 'Sikhism at a glance'.

I'm very grateful to Sardarni Narinder Kaur and S. Ram Rachpal Singh (for reviewing both, the sections on Sikhism & Christianity) and to Dr. (Prof.) Gurcharan Singh, Dr. Amarjit Singh, Washington, D.C., Dr. (Brig.) S. S. Syalee, Raja Mrigendra Singh, Ph.D. (World Religions), Mr. Edward Esteve, Dr. Jit Singh Chandan, S. Charanjit Singh Puri, S. Daljit Singh Jawa, and S. Satnam Singh Narula, all of whom have been very helpful with their suggestions. I appreciate the contributions of S. Arjan Singh Anand and his son, S. Mohinder Singh Anand, who always remind me of my own spiritual bonding with my late father.

I'm very grateful to Mrs. Saraswati Dasari, for her intelligent suggestions, encouragement and help, during various phases of writing the book. During my long association with her, I've been especially touched by her utmost sincerity, while learning from her, the lesson that service to humanity is service to God, which she practices.

I don't have adequate words of praise for Mrs. Nandita Singh, MA fine arts who holds a rare distinction of being a gold medallist through-out her college career and her husband, a renowned artist, Mr. Gurpal Singh, for the most precious gift of their dedicated efforts in designing the award winning website for Divine Power, Inc. I also appreciate the help provided by Ms Jan Guarino and Mr. Mandeep Singh for the beautiful cover designing of this book.

I thank my intellectual-critic and life-partner, Dr. Satnam Kaur, as this book may not have been possible, but for her continuous patience and ever inspiring smile, during this work, as she has done throughout our marital life. I am highly indebted for the massive support from my doting and obedient children, Punit Kaur, Gunit Singh & Pavit Singh who took time off from their schooling, to act as my 'Book-Reviewers'. I've always strived to inculcate, in them, the Spirit of serving humanity, by way of getting them involved in my literary projects, in order to leave an enduring spiritual imprint on their minds.

INDEX

Please note: At some places, the deeper meaning of the quotations from SGGS is given, instead of the plain literal. ('SGGS' : Shri Guru Granth Sahib, the Scripture of Sikh Faith).

Crucifixion of Christ
Persecuted by the rulers, he was crucified (Good Friday)
only to be resurrected on the third day (Holy Easter).

Martyrdom of Bhai Mati Das
(November 10, 1675)
He was sawed alive, and eye-witness accounts testify that the Holy
Japji Sahib Hymns were audible, from both parts.

Saint Mother Teresa
A Nobel Prize laureate, she was an epitome of selfless-service,
exemplifying non-discrimination amongst humanity.
Born in the affluent West, she chose to serve the poverty-stricken
and sick masses in the slums of distant Calcutta, India, which she
later made the headquarters of the Order she founded:
Missionaries of Charity.

Saint Puran Singh
He refused to be nominated for the Nobel Award. A Hindu by
birth, he slept hungry, in a Hindu Temple, the Priests not even
caring to share the left-overs. In contrast, he was extremely
touched by the hospitality, at a Sikh Gurdwara. He converted to
Sikhism, and served all people suffering from the dreaded leprosy,
at a hospital, he founded in Pingalwara, Punjab.

Symbol of Christianity

The 'Cross' upon which Christ died,
became the symbol of Christianity,
because Christians have seen,
in the seeming defeat of his death,
the
True Victory of Mankind.

Christian Prayer

Prayer of St. Francis

Lord, make me an instrument of Your peace;
Where there is hatred, let me sow love;
Where there is injury, pardon;
Where there is doubt, faith;
Where there is darkness, light;
Where there is sadness, joy.

O' Divine Master, grant that I may not so much seek to
be consoled as to console;
to be understood as to understand;
to be loved as to love.

For, it is in giving that we receive;
it is in pardoning that we are pardoned;
it is in dying that we are born to eternal life,

AMEN.

CHRISTIANITY
at a glance

Neither Christianity, itself, nor it's ethics can be understood in isolation from Judaism. They are 'THE INSEPARABLES'.

For Christianity began as a sect of Judaism. The Prophets of ancient Israel perceived the activity of YAHWEH in the history of their people. They saw that YAHWEH, the 'God of the Exodus', always brought oppressed people, living in bondage, to freedom and a new way of life. At different times in Israel's history, there was someone leading the Exodus.

From about 1000 B.C., Moses was succeeded by the line of kings, starting from David. The Prophets recognized the continuance of Yahweh's guidance and protection in each king, as he ascended the throne. But, not all kings were faithful, and the Prophets looked more and more towards the future, when they expected a king like David, who would be strong enough to lead the people to freedom, and to restore Israel to it's former pre-eminent position.

Founded by Jesus Christ, about A.D. 30-33, in the Judean province of Palestine (modern-day Israel State) then a part of the Roman Empire. The Bible is the Holy Book (The Old Testament, written originally in Hebrew and Aramaic, and the New Testament, in Greek).

The focus, in Christianity, is on Jesus of Nazareth, born of Virgin Mother Mary, as a Divine Gift. He proclaimed the imminent coming of the Kingdom of God on earth. He was a religious teacher in the Jewish tradition (both his parents were Jews).

After a preaching career of no more than three years, Jesus was executed by the Roman authorities (probably in 29 CE) on charges framed by some Jews, who were growing apprehensive that his claims, pertaining to being God's Son, the promised Messiah, might trigger off an insurrection which would be, eventually, suppressed by the mighty Roman Empire. This was not acceptable

7

to the Jews as it would have eroded the remaining little power and influence.

Christ's disciples, all of whom had deserted him, at his arrest, later rallied around him, and asserted that he had been raised from the grave, and testified that this symbolized, and demonstrated, that he was not only the Messiah, but also the one sent by God, to bring spiritual salvation to the whole of humanity. Within twenty years this message was preached to non-Jews, and the new religion based on it was spreading westwards throughout the Roman Empire.

Gradually, the Jewish heritage was replaced by beliefs, practices, and a church order, that owed much to the Greco Roman culture, to which most Christians now belonged. Terms like Son of God, or Lord became more popular descriptions of Jesus.

As Christianity moved further away from its parent Judaism, it began to imbibe the anti semetism of the Roman world. Jews came to be called Christ killers, and for about sixteen centuries they were persecuted, and subjected to various forms of discrimination, culminating in the great Holocaust of the 20th century.

In 313 CE, Emperor Constantine legalized the Christian religion, paving the path for it to be recognized as the State religion of the Empire, by the end of the century. Attempts were made to identify and codify the Christian beliefs at Church Councils, and through such formalities as the Nicene Creed.

The concept of Christiandom developed, with a relationship of the church and the state combining to create nations, based and ruled on Christian principles. Although they achieved some degree of harmony under the authority of the Bishop of Rome, the Pope, no form of political unity or cohesion could be arrived at.

The eastern churches, finally, rejected the supremacy of the Pope in 1054, but the most serious challenge to the remaining unity of Christendom came in the sixteenth century, when a number of people known as reformers or protestors, pioneered by a German monk, Martin Luther, questioned the pope's authority.

Their study of the Bible convinced them that the medieval church had developed a momentum of its own, often contrary to Scripture, and was in need of reform. The result was that while the Church (now designated as the Roman Catholic Church) acknowledging the Pope as its Head, remained, by far, the largest, yet many other denominations emerged.

For centuries, these reformed or protestant churches existed as rivals, but during the twentieth century a spirit of ecumenism has developed, resulting in harmony and cooperation, and sometimes even in structural unity.

Within the Christian spectrum, exist a number of groups which are particularly active in missionary work, and which place the power of the Holy Spirit, and their understanding of Christian truth above ecumenical concerns, but many regard the Pope as 'anti-Christ'. Among these are Evangelicals and Pentecostalists. Other movements, such as Jehovah's Witnesses and Latter Day Saints (the Mormons) are often considered to be outside the limits of Christianity, by many of the major denominations.

Christian worship varies from one denomination to another. It is always congregational, but the focus may be on the exposition of the Bible, or on the Last Supper, that Jesus shared with his disciples, on the night preceding his martyrdom.

Not surprisingly, ethics featured prominently in the teachings of Jesus, for they were integral and important aspect of his heritage. He often clashed with his co-religionists over the interpretations of the ethical teachings in the Torah. He did not give his followers particular precepts, but invited them to base their attitudes on the principle of love for God, and love for one's fellow human beings. Christians define 'love' in terms of Christ's own personal example. He is their role model.

For much of the span that Constantine became Emperor, Christians enjoyed favored political status and power, enabling them to influence governmental policies and programmes.

In matters of personal morality, Christians would agree that theft, murder, and adultery are wrong. With regard to isuues, such as the determination of punishment to be meted out to criminals, pacifism, abortion, and euthanasia, and regarding many other issues including cohabiting in a stable relationship outside marriage, many opposing views have emerged, in recent centuries.

There is also considerable debate as to whether Christians should use any power they may possess to impose their beliefs, in these matters, on others, by way of exercising influence on politicians and the like. In some parts of the world, there exist Christian political parties, and other pressure groups and caucuses. On the other side are those who find it impossible to endorse any political world-order, as being Christian; they are critical of all regimes and parties.

The One God is Triune : HE is present in three persons : the Father, the Son, and the Holy Spirit. God is a spiritual being, without a physical body. He is personal, and is involved with His people's lives. He created the Universe out of nothing, and He is eternal, formless, loving and perfect. Change does not have an effect on Him.

Jesus is God, the second persona in the Trinity. He is God, and man, simultaneously. He was begotten through the Holy Spirit, and was born of Virgin Mary. As per God's plan, Jesus died on the Cross-, as full sacrifice and payment, for the sins committed by mankind. On the third day he was resurrected, and was witnessed by many as having taken meals. His wounds were touched, and then he ascended to the Heaven, physically. Jesus shall return to the earth, during the end of the world, and shall establish God's kingdom, and judge the world.

The term 'Christian' was first used in Antioch in Syria, in c.35-40 CE, to designate a new religious community, there, which included both, Jewish and non-Jewish adherents. It was marked by an interesting vestigial link with Judaism, in the name 'Christian', derived from 'Christo', the Greek translation of the Hebrew title word for Messiah : 'Christos' (Acts 2:26), a Greek 'Messiah', used by Jews to designate their anticipated national savior. In this case it was applied to the prophet-teacher Jesus of Nazareth, executed in Judea, where the movement had originated, a few years earlier.

The sobriquet 'Christian' stuck as the movement further evolved, and spread. Christianity has appeared in a profusion of different forms and expressions, but allegiance to Christ is crucial to all. It is also appropriate that the word used to identify Christians is a Jewish technical term, as the roots of the movement lie deep in the life and teachings of ancient Israel, and significantly it is a Jewish term, translated into Greek. The multitudinous forms in which Christianity appears are conditioned by cultural and linguistic factors, so that translatability and transmission across cultural frontiers are leading characteristics of Christianity as a faith.

The Jewish Scriptures: The earliest Christians were Jews, well read in the scriptures of Israel, which traditionally subsisted in three categories namely the Law, the Prophets, and the Writings. Although Christianity soon developed as an overwhelmingly Gentile movement, the Christian communities continued to read the Jewish scriptures, to relate these to Christ, and to use them as an authoritative source for teaching and debate. By this means the Jewish scriptures came to be designated by the Christians as the Old Testament or Covenant, representing a stage of the divine dealings with humanity, prior to the advent of Christ.

The New Testament Writings: For the life and work of Jesus, 'the Christ', the collection of early Christian writings known as the New Testament is the crucial early source. This consists of four accounts of the ministry and teaching of Jesus, called the Gospels; a supplement to the third of the Gospels, describing the early teachings of Jesus in Jerusalem and the wider Mediterranean world, are called Acts of the Apostles; a collection of letters, the Epistles, mostly to Congregations and a few to individuals, many of which bear the name of Paul; and a work which combines several more letters with prophecies and interpretation of the history, the Apocalypse or Revelation of John.

These writings reflect the ideas and images of Jesus held in the early Christian communities, and indeed brought these communities into being, as well as giving accounts of his teachings. The special status of the New Testament writings originally derived from their association in some way with the group of followers of Jesus, known as the Apostles, who were chosen by Jesus himself. While still living, they were recognized as the founders and regulators of the Christian community, in the sense that their interpretation of his person and teachings was regarded as authoritative.

For a short but vital period during the Judaic phase (c.30-70 CE) Christianity was entirely Jewish in composition and mode of life. To a contemporary observer, the early Christian community described in the opening chapters of the Acts of the Apostles would have appeared to be one more of the seemingly infinite variations of Judaism. All its members were Jews by birth or inheritance. Their regular meeting-place was the Temple in Jerusalem, symbolic center of the nation's worship.

However, there were some distinctive features of the early Christian community's life and belief were expressed in terms of the scriptures of Israel, and the Jewish experience and aspirations. The Apostles, the chosen associates of Jesus, were the principal witnesses of the resurrection of Jesus. The resurrection was the irrefutable crowning evidence that he was the divinely appointed Messiah, the promised savior of the nation. The prophetic writings indicated that the Age to come would dawn with the arrival of the Messiah, which era had, therefore, now begun, opening the way to the moral renewal of the nation as People of God.

Through Jesus, now, people might now be forgiven their past sins and shortcomings, and become the blessed recipients of the of an overflow of divine presence and energy, the Holy Spirit, as all the Scriptures indicated.

Group worship, usually in the Church, is performed sans any secret rites and rituals. Baptism and the Lord's Supper (Communion) are the salient features. Active voluntary missionary efforts are encouraged, by the Faith.

Christians believe that Jesus is the Jewish Messiah, promised to Israel, in the Old Testament.

Eastern Christianity has a long history of persecution and disability. In early days, Christians in the eastern Mediterranean bore the fiercest attacks of the pagan Roman state, a memory kept alive by the assiduous veneration of the martyrs. Over the long centuries of Muslim rule every inducement was given to convert from the faith. Attrition became the norm, survival the goal, and fierce attachment to a glorious past, the means. Russian Christians, spared Turkish over-rule, generally thought of themselves as the defenders of their persecuted brethren; but under Soviet rule, they, too, were known to bear persecution, of varying degrees of ferocity. To its adherents, therefore, Eastern Christianity is, simply, Christianity ; their Church is not a denomination, but the Universal and Orthodox Church.

Christianity is in unanimous agreement with other religions, while advising the adherents, on a wide gamut of issues, and while suggesting remedies to the multifarious problems that afflict all mankind, in general, irrespective of religious affiliations.

Sanctification
Sanctification is achieved by God's Grace, and not due to noble deeds of man, and it must be received by deep faith. After death, all those who are saved by Jesus live eternally, with Jesus, and the others choose to Hell.

Sin
"Addictions lead to Sin and Evil leads to Suffering" is the 'creed' of all the religions. Addiction of all hues and colors is forbidden, strictly, whether it is adultery, gambling, or drug-intake or alcoholism. Exploitation of the weaker sections of the society, for satiating one's lust for carnal-instincts, power and wealth, is, also, another variety of addiction.

Though modern Christian thought advocates equality of womenfolk, in olden times, status of women in society was that of subjugation to men, in a male dominated society (as per innumerable Biblical quotations, that are too many to be listed here).

About the sin of adultery, Christianity says: "A bastard shall not enter the Congregation of the Lord"; no mention is made of the sinful act of the 'bastard' parents.

Purpose-of-Life

The ideal Purpose-of-Life has been enunciated as : "Service to Humanity ids Service to God". All craving after desires and materialistic pleasures has been relegated to the secondary position, while awarding the "superior" status to God-realization, through a daily-routine of Prayer & Meditation, that would be instrumental in ridding the aspirant of the various evils. And this would be a "blessing" for the entire lifetime. Christianity sees sin as real act of rebellion against the Only Perfect One (God).

Ceremonies, Rituals & Sacraments :

Christianity gives prominence to the sacraments. The Roman Catholic Church recognizes seven of them. Nearly all the Christians consider two of these as obligatory. They are the sacrament of Baptism and the sacrament of Eucharist.

The first deals with the initiation and purification ceremonies, and the second is the symbol of eternal sacrifice. The first is performed once in a lifetime, and the second is performed daily. Water is used in the former, while bread and wine in the latter. The bread, given as 'strength' to the believer, is symbolic of Christ's body, and wine represents Christ's blood, that was, once, poured out on Calvary, and now given for our 'sanctification'. While taking both these articles, the worshipper is supposed to inherit the nature and life of Christ, thus becoming one with him. The sacrament of marriage includes the exchange of marriage-vows, as well as of finger-rings, and is performed in the name of the Father, the Son, and the Holy Spirit. The 'day of judgment' is an important doctrine in Christianity.

Miracles:

John Locke, the great Oxford philosopher and Christian thinker (1632) said in his celebrated book 'Reasonableness of

Christianity', that the proof of the authentic nature of Christianity is the presence of the 'element of supernatural' in it: i.e., a supernatural virgin birth; a supernatural resurrection; and, a supernatural series of miracles, beginning from Christ, down through the centuries. Miracles at the famous 'Lourdes Shrine' are well known. Hundreds of these have not only been documented at the Vatican, but also testified by a verification process.

In the Holy Bible, there is mention of 'sea-dividing' (Josh 3:9-17), the 'sun standing still' (Josh 10:12-14), 'man disappearing into the sky in a chariot of fire (II Kings 2:11), serpents (in Gen. 3:1-40) and asses (in Num. 22:28-30) 'talking as humans', 'axe-heads that float' (II Kings 6:4-7) and Jonah 'surviving in the stomach of a whale' (Jonah 1:17) and in a worm eaten gourd (Jon 3:6-7). Although the doors were shut, Jesus came and stood among them. John 20:26

Jesus performed miracles which are supposed to have become the mainstay of his divinity. He cured a leper (Matthew 8:3), cast out devil from a Greek girl (Mark 7:25-30), cured a blind man (Mark 9: 2-10), turned water into wine (John 2;1-11), fed one man's food to thousands (Mark 6:30-44), spoke to the wind and the waves (Mark 4:35-41), made a crippled person walk (John 5:1-9), brought back the dead to life (John 11:38-44). It was on the basis of his miracles of Tetra (wonders) , Dunameis (mighty acts) and Semeia (signs) that in 451 A.D., the Council of Chalcedon declared Jesus as "God in human form".

But, we also find that similar miracles have, also, been performed by other Christian and Jewish Prophets, and yet they are not considered as great as Christ ! For instance, Elisha fed 100 people with only 20 barley loafs (II Kings 4:44), cured Naaman of leprosy (II Kings 5:14), and cured a blind young man (II Kings 16-17). Ravens brought bread and flesh to Elijah (I Kings 17:16). Elijah raised a child from the dead (I Kings 17:22, II Kings 13:21, II Kings 4:34).

Although Christians attach great significance to Christ's miracles, Jesus, himself, is said to have admitted that miracles can be performed by non-Christians, disbelievers, and false Prophets. In

Matthew 24:24, he says: "for there shall be false Christs and false Prophets and shall show signs and wonders".

Even retention of hair has been illustrated as having great and miraculous source of power, according to the following Biblical quotes, hitherto not highlighted in the Christian world.

Details of Samson's birth and the miraculous powers of hair have been given in the Chapter on Miracle. During a battle, in which Samson killed thousands, single-handedly, "Samson was tired and weary, but God sent water gushing from a rock. Samson drank some and felt strong again". He called it the 'Caller-Spring' or 'Enhakkore'. It is located at Jawbone, in Israel (Judges 15: 19).

Festivals :

The following are the significant days in Christianity:
December 8 is celebrated as the Day of Immaculate Conception, when Jesus was said to have been conceived.
December 25 is Christmas, celebrates the birth of Jesus.

Holy Thursday is celebrated in reminiscence of the night, prior to the Crucifixion, when Jesus had the Last Supper, with his disciples, and is said to have pardoned the traitors, who backstabbed him.
Good Friday is when Jesus was nailed on The Cross; it is 'Good' because he died to redeem all the sinners.
Easter, in April, is the day of resurrection, when Christ is believed to have risen from his grave, where he rested for three days after his crucifixion.

Asceticism and Monasticism
The Roman Catholic history is one of survival of religious orders, in their present form, where individual-monasteries, of men and women, began in the fourth century Egypt.

Monotheism, Polytheism
The competing systems of religious belief that only one god exists or that many gods exist. Bible students often argue on the basis of biblical evidence that Israel in the first centuries of her life as a

people did not have a monotheistic system of belief: indeed, that Moses' tradition does not appear in that kind of category. To support the accuracy of this statement, they examine the central text in the Old Testament for defining Israel's belief about God: the Ten Commandments.

The first commandment stipulates a fundamental tenet in Israel's belief system: "Thou shalt have no other gods before me" (Ex. 20:3). That requirement for participation in Israel's community of faith does not assert that serving other gods before one serves the Lord would be foolish since no other gods exist. It assumes quite to the contrary that other gods do exist. It asserts that, even though the other gods exist, the people who follow the Mosaic Commandments shall not embrace any of those other gods as gods who compete for the loyalty of the people. The Lord who brought Israel out of the land of Egypt will allow no compromise in the loyalty of the people. That assertion assumes the existence of other false gods who could call for loyalty and commitment from the Lord's people. That kind of belief system is commonly called henotheism.

Teachings Of Jesus Christ

"Never man spake like this man" with such authority (John 7:46; compare Matt. 7:29). His teachings were about "the Father," what He wanted, what He was like, what He would do for His creation. Jesus' teachings required absolute obedience and love for God and the kingdom of God. He dared claim that the kingdom had begun in His ministry but would not be culminated until Christ's final coming. Until that coming, Christians were to live in the world by the ethical injunctions He gave (Matt. 5-7) and in the kind of love He had shown and commanded (John 14-16). To help earthly people understand heavenly things, He spoke in parables. These parables were from realistic, real-life settings. They were about the kingdom of God—what it was like, what was required to live in it, what was the meaning of life according to its teachings, what the kingdom promised. One of the promises of the kingdom was that the King would return and rule in it.

The 10 Commandments : Deuteronomy 5.1-21

God addressed the Israelites, thus:

1) I am the lord, your God who delivered you out of slavery in Egypt. Do not worship any God except me. If you reject me I shall punish your families for three or four generations. But if you love me I shall be kind to your families for thousands of generations

2) Do not worship idols that look like anything in the sky, or on earth, or in the ocean under the earth.

3) Do not misuse my Name; I will punish anyone doing so.

4) No one is to work on Sabbath day, for it belongs to me; work for six days, but not on the seventh.

5) Respect your parents and you will live a long time in the land I am giving you.

6) Do not commit murder.

7) Be faithful in marriage.

8) Do not steal.

9) Do not tell lies about others.

10) Do not covet what belongs to another, be it another's spouse, land, home, authority, gold, cash, slave, or cattle.

Summary

Christ is the way to God. His way of being in the world was a way of obedience, faithfulness, and service. The earliest Christians saw who He was in what He did. In the great deed of the cross they saw the salvation of the world. The inspired writers offered no physical descriptions of the earthly Jesus. The functional way the New Testament portrays Him is found in the statement that He was a man "who went about doing good" (Acts 10:38). The good that He did came into dramatic conflict with the evil all mankind has done. This conflict saw Him crucified, but a Roman soldier saw in this crucified One (the) Son of God (Mark 15:39). God did not "suffer thine Holy One to see corruption" (Acts 2:27). With the one shattering new act since creation, God raised Jesus from the dead.

Glancing toward the future, one might say that the concerns of Christians will be mainly related to their relations with other Christians belonging to several denominations, the environment, racism, and the ministry of women, attitudes towards and relations with adherents of other Faiths. This is primarily a Western agenda; Christians in Asia and Africa would have different perspectives.

Symbol of Sikhism

THE KHANDA

There are two swords on the sides, symbolizing temporal and spiritual powers, and the double-edged sword in the middle represents a unity of these two sovereign powers. The circle symbolizes the infinitude of eternal God, who has no beginning or end.

Sikh Prayer

You are the Lord, we pray to You.
You have favored us with our being and our body.

You are our mother and father;
we are Your progeny.
In Your Grace, lie many comforts and luxuries.

Nobody can ascertain the limits of Your Glory.
O' Lord, You are higher than the highest.
The whole creation rests upon Your support.

Whatever has sprung from You,
follows Your command.

God, Your ways are mysterious.
Pleads Nanak : "I'm your loving, ardent devotee".

S I K H I S M
at a glance

SIKHISM is a monotheistic religion that was revealed to Guru Nanak, the Sikh Prophet around 1501 C.E. It presents a unique message of love and tolerance for all humanity. It brought about a revolution by awakening many gullible, ignorant masses that were being exploited by the Hindu priestly class, the Brahmins, and were oppressed by the tyranny of the Moslem invaders, the Mughals and the Afghans. Through the realization that all human beings are equal in the eyes of God, the subjugated masses rebelled against the status quo, stemming the tide of oppression for the first time in 3000 years of South Asian history. The Sikh Prophets, using the Divine Revelation of God's Word as their inspiration, changed the course of history of South Asia, and (by implication) of the history of the world.

In order to achieve success in their noble mission, the Sikh Gurus practiced what they preached. They sacrificed their own lives and embraced martyrdom. Their innumerable disciples emulated their example by becoming equally valiant and by laying down their lives for righteousness. The entire history of Sikhism is replete with sagas of Martyrdom, for nurturing the sapling, planted by the Gurus. The postulates of Sikhism emphasize that the ultimate goal of a human-being is not a vision of God that culminates in re-absorption of the individual into the absolute reality, but the emergence of a race of God-conscious people, who remain earth-aware and thus operate in the mundane world of the phenomena, with the object of transforming and spiritualizing it into a higher and more abundant plane of existence. As the Sikh scripture declares, "The God-conscious person is animated with an intense desire to do good in this world."

Miracles
Miracles abounded, in the life and times of the Founder, Guru Nanak through the Tenth Master, Guru Gobind Singh. Gurdwaras are now erected at the places associated with these miracles, where the occurrences can be verified, today. **The Indelible Imprint**: One of the most acclaimed of these is Panja Sahib, Pakistan, where Guru Nanak's hand has left an indelible imprint on a rock. In

village Batala, Punjab State. **The Wall that wouldn't fall** : A weak wall, erected to kill Guru Nanak, while he would sit near it, stands even today, after five centuries. **Stone as Wax**: Guru Nanak's figurine has been framed in a rock, as if it were wax. Located in Ladakh region of Jammu & Kashmir, India. **Bitter into Sweet**: One branch of a tree gives sweet fruit, as a result of Guru Nanak's glance, while all other branches continue retaining their bitter nature. Location: Pilibhit, Uttar Pradesh in India. **The Mobile mosque**: A plate bearing reference to this incident, related with the visit of Guru Nanak, is preserved, reverentially, in Mecca, Saudi Arabia. Innumerable other miracles cannot be listed here, for paucity of print-space.

It is amazing to note that some two centuries before scientists had even discovered the telescope, and none could even dream of visiting the space, Guru Nanak, through Revelation and spiritual powers, determined that many other planets, suns and moons existed. Furthermore, he conclusively elaborated upon the complexities of the Creation of the Universe, as written in the Sikh Scripture. It is quite a coincidence that as we write this, newspapers in America corroborate his statement, made over five centuries, ago, regarding the possibility of the existence of many suns and moons", and of life on other planets.

The GURU & The SIKH
The founder of Sikhism, Guru Nanak Dev, was born in 1469 A.D., at Village Talwandi, near Lahore (now in Pakistan). Nanak was greatly inclined towards spirituality, even at that tender young age.
Guru, in Sikh terminology, means a Prophet and a world-teacher. Sikhism is a prophetic religion based on a definitive revelation like Semitic religions of the west, and it, therefore, can be clearly be contra-distinguished from the eastern religions of Hinduism, Buddhism and Taoism, which have an anonymous mysticism as their source of validity.
Guru Nanak's encounter with God is described, metaphorically, in the *Janamsakhis* (textual-narrations, pertaining to his birth-lore) in the following words: "As God willed, Nanak, his devotee, was escorted to His presence, to the divine presence, and then a cup filled with Liquid of Immortality was given to him, accompanied by the command: Nanak, pay attention. This is the cup of holy

adoration of my Name; drink it. I am with you, and you do I bless and exalt. Go, rejoice in my Name, the Name of God, and preach to others to do the same. Let this be your calling."

The term "Sikh" originates from ancient Pali texts, where the word "Sikho," is used for a searcher of truth. A Sikh of Guru Nanak also strives to destroy the wall of nescience that separates him or her from Truth. "How will the Truth become known and how will the wall of nescience be pierced," asks Guru Nanak in the first chapter of the Sikh scripture. Then, answers: "It is possible, by following the Will of God and by being in tune with the Cosmic Law, will be able to grasp Reality".

The Sikh Gurus wrote their revelations in various languages and dialects so they would be accessible to people without any intermediaries. Through this act, Sikhism rejected the priestly class of the time, which tried to control the religious practices of the people by writing all religious texts in Sanskrit, an ancient language that is difficult to understand. For the first time, a religion in the Eastern world offered access to God without the priestly class.

To understand the emergence and expansion of Sikhism, in true perspective, it is imperative that the prevailing conditions (and their ramifications) be studied.
Islam and Hinduism were the two predominant faiths in the Indian subcontinent, when Guru Nanak received his ministry from God. Hindus were absorbed in practices that are strongly condemned by Sikhism: idol-worship; female infanticide; sati (forcible burning of a widow on her husband's funeral-pyre); "devadasi" system, where girls who had attained puberty would be used to satiate the carnal instincts of the Brahmin priests.
Polygamy was rampant; a man could have as many wives as he desired, and innumerable concubines. Women widows could not remarry. Young teen-aged girls were marrying off forcibly. Women had no access to education. Animals and even humans, especially virgin, teenaged girls approaching puberty would be considered "most acceptable to the presiding-deity" of a tribe or of a family.

Sacrificing the life of a householder, after attaining the age of seventy-five was considered to be a preferred way of life for the Hindus. They would renounce society and take refuge in forests, mountains or caves for the remainder of their lives. The Hindu society was stratified based on caste into four classes; the lowest one was considered to be "untouchables." Even today, these "untouchables," the Dalits, are trapped in perpetual poverty and do not have access to the same human rights as the upper class Hindus. Hundreds-of-thousands of Hindus were proselytized to Islam with the use of the sword, where the 'options' were : Islam or death.

Basic TENETS & THEOLOGY

Sikhism rejects, outright, the aforementioned practices, prevalent in Hinduism and Islam. Sikhism, however, being a monotheistic faith and a reveled religion shares many similarities with the Semitic traditions such as Judaism, Christianity and Islam. However, Sikhism does not believe in the doctrine of Original Sin; nor does it believe in a Heaven or a Hell. Sikhism preaches that we are rewarded or punished, according to our actions in this lifetime; we reap what we sow. Human life is precious because it is our opportunity to meet God, while living on this earth. Through good actions and by endeavoring to love humanity, we achieve Self-Realization. God is not a distant reality; God resides within us and pervades the entire creation. God is, both, Immanent and Transcendent. "Some sing your praises thinking you are Transcendent; others praise you thinking you are Immanent".

Sikhs are distinct from Hindus and Muslims, from all angles, including religious practices, ceremonies, festivals, social customs and traditions. The Sikh scripture declares, "Guru Nanak [the Sikh Prophet] recognizes no authority, no doctrine, except that directly revealed to him by God." *(SGGS* page 599).

Since the Gurus wanted to have an enduring impact, and not just a superficial one, it took 10 Gurus a period of over 250 years to "condition the soul and spirit" of their followers, to face the tyrant rulers and the barbaric intruders with courage and fortitude. Cowardice and indifference was effectively replaced with courage and bravery. The basic tenets of Sikh Faith are prayer and meditation, honest living, generosity, compassion and sharing, humility and patience. Other important planks on which rests the Sikh faith are: equality of all religions, universal harmony, peace and tolerance. Service to humanity has been emphasized. Hair is a symbol of saintliness, and a reminder of God's design. It's a must for a Sikh man and a woman to retain unshorn hair, and to refrain from adultery, and use of drugs and other intoxicants like alcohol, cocaine, tobacco, opium, marijuana etc. Lust, too, has been termed an addiction. It is a major religious and spiritual diktat, for a Sikh not to live on alms or donations. Furthermore, a Sikh considers it to be a psychological trauma, and a social stigma, accepting monetary benefits, which one has not worked to earn.

Repudiation of Rituals

In Sikhism, there is no place for idolatry (statue, icons, symbols, or photographs) or human-worship. Ritualism and superficial fanfare related to ceremonies has been denounced. Superstitious beliefs related to so-called specific auspicious days and dates have been negated. The Gurus command that all days have been made by God; therefore, all are equally auspicious; all humanity is created by the Lord; therefore all are equal. The time when one remembers God is auspicious and the place where one remembers God is sacred. No time or place can be sacred in itself.

Non-Violence

Sikhs are a peace-loving people. Non-violence, which enforces a strict prohibition against the use of arms under any circumstances, however, has no place in Sikhism. The Sikh Prophet, Guru Gobind Singh, declares, "When all peaceful means fail, to take up the sword is a lawful imperative, to contain the oppressor". He further states, "I would confront and oppose that what is evil, to destroy it or to subdue it, or die fighting against it, with dignity."

The fifth and the ninth Gurus were Martyrs; the four teenaged sons of the 10th Guru were Martyrs (the younger ones, aged 7 and 9 were bricked alive; the older ones, 15 and 17, performed the supreme sacrifice on the battlefield, facing ruthless seasoned warriors); and they embraced death, as did innumerable of their followers, for upholding their birthright of the choice of practicing the religion of their choice. They preferred death to a life of slavery and subjugation. There is no sign of 'suffering' on the faces of the Martyrs; no repentance, no regrets.

The SCRIPTURE
The teachings of Sikh Gurus and Saints, in the form of poetic compositions that have been compiled in the Sikh Scripture, Sri Guru Granth Sahib (SGGS). This 1430 page volume is reverentially placed on an elevated pedestal in the Gurdwara (Sikh Church). The Holy Book has been written, compiled and edited by the Gurus, during their lifetimes. It is noteworthy that out of all the scriptures of religions of the world, it is the only scripture written by the same person who received the Revelation.

The Tenth and the last Sikh Prophet, Guru Gobind Singh, transferred his authority to the Sikh scripture and to the collectivity of the committed Sikhs, known as the Khalsa. This is the condominium of Guru Granth and Guru Khalsa Panth. The spirit of the Ten Sikh Prophets resides in the mystic body of the Khalsa, while their light resides in the Sikh scripture. The Sarbat Khalsa, an assemblage of representative Sikhs from all over the world, takes major decisions affecting the Sikh nation in consonance with the teachings of the Sikh Gurus enshrined in Guru Granth Sahib. The Sarbat Khalsa has the responsibility to keep the Sikh personal law dynamic and address new issues as they arise.

The 10th Guru, in his wisdom, did not deem it appropriate to include his own autobiography and his poetic encomiums for God, in the SGGS, at par with his predecessors. There is a lot of controversy about the contents of the Dasam Granth, and an overwhelming majority of Sikh saints, theologians, scholars, and preachers hold the firm conviction that several 'additions' were made to his original works, by vested interests, with an ulterior motive of neutralizing the worldview that the Sikhs have a unique and distinct identity, thereby wrongly attempting to present the Sikhs as part of Hinduism, trying to merge a minority with the majority.

'GURDWARA' (House of Worship)
Gurdwara, which literally means "a door to the Guru," is the focal point for all Sikh congregations. Guru Nanak, the first Sikh Prophet, established the institution to organize Sikhs on a local

level. Since the Sikh doctrine does not allow separation between spiritual and temporal affairs, all political movements affecting Sikhs have been launched from Gurdwaras. Some of the best examples are the Sikh non-violent fight against British aggression in the 1920s and against Indira Gandhi's military rule, known as the Emergency, in 1970s. Even though the latter affected the entire country, out of a country of almost billion people, only the Sikhs, who are just two percent of the total population, found courage to oppose tyranny.

There is no ordained priestly class in Sikhism. All Sikhs are expected to read prayers, sing hymns and perform other services. Both women and men can participate in all services and can occupy any administrative positions. As a mark of respect, all devotees must enter the Gurdwara, after taking off their footwear, and with their heads covered. They bow in front of the Sikh scripture and then sit down to listen to the devotional hymns. It is important to note that the act of genuflection in front of the Sikh scripture is not idol worship. A Sikh bows to the message contained in the scripture and not to a book. Genuflection in front of the Sikh scripture indicates submission to the Word of God. Later, the Congregation stands up in prayer, and at the conclusion of the services partakes of *langar*, which is any type of food prepared with love and devotion by the community. The tradition of *langar* was started by Guru Nanak and was institutionalized by Guru Amar Dass, the third Sikh Prophet. All were required to partake *langar* before interviewing the Guru. Before this policy was put into effect, many Hindu Brahmins would come and meet the Guru but not eat with the "lower-caste" women and men in the Guru's congregation. This bold initiative ended all hypocrisy and confirmed equality between all humanity, as all were forced to eat together. Even a Mughal Emperor, Akbar, partook *langar* while sitting on the floor with common people before he could meet with the Guru. Langar inspires and promotes the spirit of disinterested action, *sewa*, in a Sikh and, therefore, must be cooked by the community and cannot be catered from a restaurant. By catering the food, an artificial distinction between the rich and the poor is created. Such a distinction repudiates the very purpose of *langar* and is antithetical to Sikhism. The Gurdwara services are performed on all occasions, whether birth, naming, graduation, commencement of a business-venture, during baptism, during wedding, thanksgiving or during sad occasions such as death. The entire Congregation, without distinction of class or creed, enjoys equal status, and all are required to sit on the floor to partake of the holy food. No Gurdwara, anywhere in the world (and there are several thousands of them) has been recorded as having been "closed" or "sold." This is a very unique aspect of the followers of Sikhism, who are famous for sacrificing their all for the welfare of humanity.

Contributions of the 10 SIKH GURUS

As it has been asserted before, the Sikh Scripture declares that the Ten Sikh Gurus were a manifestation of one Divine Light that passed on from one prophet to the next. Even though they changed bodies, the light remained intact and they preached the same message though out the 250 years of their sojourn on this earth.

The Founder of Sikhism, *Guru Nanak Dev*, brought about a revolution in the eastern world. He opposed tyranny and exploitation. He rebelled against futile practices, empty rituals, and superstitions, as already described before. God sent him as a Prophet to reveal Sikhism to the Humanity. Guru Nanak was probably the first Human Rights activist known to the Eastern world. The ruling emperor, Babur, imprisoned him when he opposed tyranny of the invader. The three basic tenets of Sikhism, as declared by Guru Nanak, are: (1) earn your livelihood with honesty, (2) constantly remember God through devotion and activism and (3) share your earnings with the needy. The Guru, who was exceedingly tolerant of other faiths, embraced the entire humanity as the children of one God.

Guru Angad Dev, the second Sikh Prophet, gave definitive shape to a new alphabet, Gurmukhi, that was to replace all existing scripts. The new script was easy to read and the common people, without the use of any intermediaries, could now read and understand Guru Nanak's message. He also strengthened Sikh congregations and preached God revelation relentlessly.

Guru Amar Das, the third Sikh Prophet, was a great defender of women's rights. Over thirty percent women preachers were appointed to preach the message of Sikhism. He also appointed women bishops. He institutionalized the Sikh tradition of Langar or community kitchen and enforced equality in all Sikh congregations. He encouraged widow remarriage and banned the horrific practice of sati, where women are forced to be burned with the funeral pyre of their dead husbands.

Guru Ram Das, the fourth Sikh Prophet, founded the spiritual Sikh capital, Amritsar, and started work on the world-famous Golden-Temple, to emphasize upon the spiritual way of living. His hymns, as recorded in the Sikh scripture, have a breathtaking theme of humility.

Guru Arjan Dev, the fifth Sikh Prophet, was a literary-giant, who undertook the work to compile the Sikh scripture. He included the hymns of Hindu and Muslim Saints, without discrimination, in the Sikh scripture. He was martyred for refusing to embrace Islam. The extent of barbaric-torture was such that he was boiled in a cauldron containing water, and hot sand poured upon his head, during scorching summers. Yet, he prayed blissfully, his face radiant.

Guru Hargobind, the sixth Sikh Prophet, was groomed by Guru Arjan to become a warrior-saint. He implemented Guru Nanak's doctrine of double-sovereignty that deems spiritual and temporal affairs are both equally important. A Sikh must strive to excel both in spiritually and temporally, always subordinating politics to ethics. The Guru created the Sikh seat of sovereignty, the Akaal Takhat, which is comparable to the Vatican. However, the head of the Akaal Takhat is just a mouthpiece of the Sikh commonwealth and all of his directives must be a result of decisions taken by the Khalsa Panth, the committed Sikhs all over the world.

Guru Har Rai, the seventh Sikh Prophet, was ordered by Guru Hargobind to maintain an army to fight oppression and to continue his mission of preaching the word of God. Arms were to be used as a last resort, when all peaceful means of reaching a resolution has failed. He pioneered Ayurvedic free health care.

Guru Harkrishan, the eighth Sikh Prophet, was appointed Guru when he barely five years old, he led the masses with grit and determination, displaying rare spiritual-acumen, wisdom and sagacity. He departed from the mortal world when only eight, proving that age has no correlation with spiritual power that is God's Gift, bestowed upon whomsoever God is Gracious. This also is an excellent example of equality, bestowed by Sikh doctrine, on all human being, men, women and children.

Guru Tegh Bahadur, the ninth Sikh Prophet, is one of the greatest defenders of freedom of conscience ever known to humankind. He preached against the Hindu caste system and repudiated the superiority of the Hindu priestly class, the Brahmins. When the Brahmins were being proselytized to Islam and came to him for help, he gave them a helping hand, and embraced martyrdom. Long before Voltaire was to say, I might not believe in what you say but I will fight till death for your right to say it, he the Guru showed the world that freedom of practice was a cherished gift that ought to be defended. The Guru was a great warrior, but he gave his life peacefully.

Guru Gobind Singh, the tenth and the last Sikh Prophet, gave up everything in his fight against oppression. He sacrificed his four sons, his parents and gave his own life while preaching the message of love. "Hear ye all, I proclaim the truth, only those who love will find God". The Guru was a prolific writer, a poet, a great warrior, a musician, a chef, and had innumerable other talents. His greatest accomplishment is his non-attachment to this world and his ordination committed Sikh, the Khalsa.

The VAISAAKHI of 1699 : Beginning of A Revolutionary era

The manner in which Guru Gobind Singh gave proof of his thorough knowledge of the art of dramaturgy on the Baisakhi day is fairly well known. He asked for a 'head'; then a brave one offered his head; he was taken inside a tent, and the Guru returned with a blood-soaked sword, asking for another head; the audience was stunned; he repeated the call, four times. Finally, he brought out the five, alive, to the amazement of the assemblage. The five were then administered, what is known as the Baptism of the Double-edged Sword (khande di pahul), and were then knighted as Singhs, the Five Beloved Ones, the first members of the Order of the Khalsa, into which the Guru himself begged to be admitted, and was initiated as the sixth. On this day, a milestone in Sikh history, Guru Gobind Singh transfigured Sikhs by giving them their modern form which includes the five articles of faith that Sikhs wear : (1) unshorn hair, (2) a small wooden comb for the hair, (3) a steel bracelet which signifies a Reality with no beginning and no end, (4) a ceremonial sword indicative of resolve and commitment to justice, and (5) knee-length under-shorts in keeping with the disciplined life-style of a Sikh. Guru Gobind Singh proclaimed a formal code of conduct that forbids adultery and promiscuous sexual behavior, use of drugs and intoxicants, cutting of hair from any part of one's body, female infanticide and consumption of sacrificial meat. Hair, being sacred, was to be kept covered at all times. This required wearing of turbans and scarves, which are also signs of sovereignty.

Ceremonies & Festivals

It is said within the Sikh faith that there are four important events in any individual's life: Birth, Amrit, Marriage, and Death. The significance of birth and death in ones life are obvious. "Amrit', the Initiation ceremony, marks the commencement of 'the journey', symbolizing the aspirant's first step as per the Sikh 'way of life'. Those who have taken Amrit are called the Khalsa. 'Anand Karaj' or marriage is another significant ceremony. It is a public commitment by two Sikhs to walk on the path of Guru Nanak throughout their lives. The marriage ceremony becomes a spiritual journey undertaken by two lovers of righteousness, striving to achieve Self-Realization.

All other ceremonies, whether child-naming, graduation, starting a business-venture or employment are, inevitably, marked by a gathering of relations and friends, at a Gurdwara. Holy hymns are recited and Langar is served to the guests.

The major festivals of the Sikhs are "Hola Mohalla," which is celebrated in March, to observe the change of season, by indulging in sports and revelry, and "Baisakhi," which has already been described. "Diwali," in November, is celebrated to mark the occasion when the sixth Guru secured the release of 52 kings from the prison of India's Mughal Emperor, Jehangir.

A Brief Sketch of SIKH History

In 1710, the Sikhs set up a republic in the heartland of the Moghul empire in India under the leadership of Baba Banda Singh Bahadur, wherein they gave the land to tillers in a feudal society, proclaimed equality of all people as citizens of a state, and

31

declared that power emanated from, and justly belonged to the people and not to a hereditary privileged class.

For fifty years, under the most callous and terrible persecutions, where the aim was complete genocide, the Sikhs not only refused to submit to the cruelty of the oppressive Muslim regime, but refused to abandon their cry: "We want liberty or death"! And in the end, once again, they had their liberty. Sikh supremacy was then established in the form of 'Sarbat-Khalsa', the Sikh Commonwealth, and then it slided into the form of the Sikh Empire, which was called the 'Sarkar-i-Khalsa', from the middle of the eighteenth century to the middle of the nineteenth century.

The Sikh Empire then extended from the Jamuna River, the heartland of India, to the modern frontiers of Afghanistan, and from Indus to the Little Tibet, the confines of China. It was the middle of the nineteenth century when the British perfidiously attacked the Sikh Commonwealth, after engineering Sikh palace intrigue, by bribing the Hindu Generals of the Sikh army and the Hindu dominated civil government at Lahore. During the fierce Anglo-Sikh wars, the Sikhs, as a historian says, "brought the British and their Hindu mercenaries to their knees every time." In pre-British India, the powerful Sikh Emperor, Maharajah Ranjit Singh, is renowned for having sanctioned grants of cash, gold, and land, for Hindu Temples, Christian Churches, and Muslim Mosques. He had, under his employ, European courtiers and generals, besides people from all religions and races, in India

In the years preceding 1947, the Sikhs played an active role during India's struggle for freedom, for which their active cooperation was enlisted by the Congress Party, which was spearheading the movement, under the stewardship of Mahatma Gandhi. At this juncture, promises pertaining to Sikh identity, representation, and autonomy were made by the Congress Party. The Sikhs believed these promises, and plunged head-on into the arena. Out of the 2,175 martyrs for India's freedom, 1,557, or 75% were Sikhs. Out of 2,646 sent to Andaman's for life sentence, for asking the British to quit India, 2,147 or 80% were Sikhs. Out of the 127 Indians who were sent to the gallows by the British, 92 or 80% were Sikhs. It is recorded in the official British records that whenever the Sikhs were taken to the execution room to be hanged, they were given a chance to apologize and have their life saved, but they preferred dignified death rather than slavery.

Ever-since independence in 1947, persistent, calculated, well planned and regular attempts have been made by the majority community, on the cultural and political levels, not only to disintegrate the Sikh people, but also to weaken them, economically. Even other minorities (Christians and Muslims) in India have been subjected to maltreatment at the hands of the majority. The promise about framing a Constitution with the consent of the Sikhs, was broken three years later in 1950. Nothing was included therein that may have even the remotest semblance to the fulfillment of the Sikhs' demand for autonomy, within the framework of the Constitution. Thus, the Sikhs had been tricked into giving up their right to sovereignty, after playing a pivotal role in attaining independence for India. A constitution was framed paving the way for a highly centralized government, in the hands of the majority community, completely denying the Sikh religious identity, and political sovereignty.

Continued frustration due to unfulfilled promises made by the Indian government in 1947, led the Sikhs to start a peaceful movement, resulting in several thousands filling the jails, over a span of quarter a century. To crush the non-violent independence movement, the government deployed ruthless tactics. In retaliation to the injustice meted out, this agitation assumed the form of Sikh independence movement, to breakaway from the Union of India. In 1984, an army operation was launched, on the Golden Temple and 37 other Sikh shrines, killing several thousand Sikhs. Over 200,000 innocent Sikhs were killed in the aftermath of this operation, and thousands are still languishing in jails, without trial. The irony of the situation is that even after 16 years, several thousand Sikh widows, sitting in the slums of Delhi, are still awaiting justice, while the killers were given Ministerial berths. The Indian State has subdued all attempts of Amnesty Intl., and local Human Rights groups like the People's Commission.

Section 1

The ONLY One

****

*One who <u>fails</u> to see God, 'everywhere',
can <u>never</u> see Him, 'anywhere'.*

****

God's mercy is bound up with His covenant with Israel. He is merciful to them because He chose them (Ex. 33:19; 2 Kings 13:23; Isa. 54:10, 63:7). God's mercy is never just a feeling but is expressed by His action: providing for Israel in the wilderness (Neh. 9:19; Isa. 49:10) and delivering her from enemies (Pss. 69:16-21; 79:8-11; Isa. 30:18; Jer. 42:11-12). When Israel turned from God, He showed no pity (Isa. 9:17; 27:11; Jer. 13:14; 16:5; Hos. 1:6-8; 2:4). On the other hand, He is a forgiving God and shows mercy to a penitent people (Pss. 25:4-7; 40:11-12; 51:1-4; Prov. 28:13-14; Isa. 54:7; 55:7; Lam. 3:31-33; Dan. 9:9; Mic. 7:19; Hab. 3:2).

The covenant of God's mercy is to be established between him and the family of Noah, Gen. v. 18. A male and female of all kinds of animals that could not live in the waters to be brought into the ark, vv. 19, 20. Noah is commanded to provide food for their sustenance, v. 21; and punctually follows all these directions, v. 22.

The inhabitants of Sodom were sinners, and exceedingly wicked, and their profligacy was of that kind which luxury produces; they fed themselves without fear, and they acted without shame. Lot however was, through the mercy of God, preserved from this contagion: he retained his religion; and this supported his soul and saved his life, when his goods and his wife perished.

If thou doest well—That which is right in the sight of God, shalt thou not be accepted? Does God reject any man who serves him in simplicity and godly sincerity? But if thou doest not well, can wrath and indignation against thy righteous brother save thee from the displeasure under which thou art fallen? On the contrary, have recourse to thy Maker for mercy;

There is a sense in which nobody doeth well (Isaiah 64:6) and that we are only acceptable to God, by His Grace (Eph.2:8:9)

God is an *experience* of affirmation of Hope and Peace, of a blissful Radiance and Fragrance. *God is serene tranquility.*

God is the Paramount Power, the Insurmountable. He is beyond the experiences of Life & Death, of Joy & Sorrow, of Victory & Defeat. And, *God* is beyond the realms of Human Knowledge and Comprehension. He is attainable by Virtue of His Own Grace (if that is forthcoming from Him) being bestowed on a devotee. He cannot be reached by persistence & penance. Meditation is the Sunlit-Path to the Glorious Destination. God is Omnipotent, Omnipresent & Omniscient. He is all pervasive, in creations and creatures, in all the mass and matter, in space and in water, on land and in the air. He is, in essence, in each particle, and in each atom. Therefore, the inference is that God is Transcendental & Immanent, both, at once, simultaneously. Before the Creation was effected, God was present, all by Himself, in a self-absorbed state of being.

He has no form, no shape, no color; God is beyond the three qualities. They alone understand Him, O Nanak, with whom He is pleased.[283 SGGS].

God is beyond the limitations of form or shape, or of social class or race. These humans believe that He is distant; but He is quite obviously and apparently very close (in fact He resides within each creature). He enjoys His presence in every heart, and no filth sticks to Him, and He is blemishless. He is the blissful and infinite Primal Lord; His Light is all pervading. Among all divine beings, He is the most divine, Creator-architect, Rejuvenator of all. How can Nanak's single tongue worship and adore Him? He is the eternal, imperishable Entity. One whom He unites with the True Guru — such a person's generations are redeemed. All His servants serve Him, and Nanak is the most humble servant at His door. [1096 SGGS]

Romans 3, 4

"Does God belong only to the Jews ?
Isn't He also the God of Gentiles ?
YES, He is.
There is only One God, and he accepts Gentiles as well as Jews,
simply because of their Faith."

Isaiah 45:5
"I am the Lord, and there is none else. There is no God besides me".

Romans 10:11, 12, 13
"The Scripture say that no one who has faith shall be disappointed, no
matter if that person is a Jew or a Gentile. There is only one Lord,
and he is generous to everyone who asks for his help. All who call out
to the Lord will be saved'.

God is One, His Name is Truth, He is the Creator, He is the Fearless One, He does not bear animosity towards anyone, He is beyond the cycle of birth and death, and He is the Benevolent Grace. [1 SGGS]

As much as the Word of God is in the mind, so much is His melody; as much as the form of the universe is, so much is His body. He is the tongue, and He is the nose. Do not speak of any other. My Lord and Master is One (GOD). He is the One and Only; He is the One alone, proclaims Nanak. [350 SGGS]

The various gods and goddesses, in various religions and cultures are, in reality, only mere manifestations of the One and ONLY God. He Himself is the Doer of deeds. [908 SGGS]

The One and Only Creator of the Universe is All-pervading. All shall once again merge into the One. His One Form has one, and many colors; He leads all according to His One Word. [1310 SGGS]

Describe the Lord as the One, the One and Only. How rare are those who know the taste of this essence. The Glories of the Lord of the Universe cannot be known, proclaims Nanak, He is totally amazing and wonderful! [299 SGGS]

The emphasis is on the message of One GOD. Hence, the various manifestations of the Powers of GOD cannot be misconstrued as being God. They only represent certain attributes of GOD, which emanate from Him, and could never be an independent 'persona' or entity.

Attributes of God: God has distinctive qualities that summarize what He is like. God's *glory* refers to the weight or influence He carries in the universe and to the overwhelming brilliance when He appears to people (Ex. 16:7-10; Isa. 6:3; Eph. 1:12-17; Heb. 1:3). It is His presence in all His sovereign power, righteousness, and love. Sometimes the Bible describes the glory of God as a physical manifestation. Sometimes it is a spiritual perception as in a sense of tremendous awe before God. We see the glory of God when we are deeply impressed with a sense of His presence and power. Wisdom is manifest in the balance God created in nature; living in balance is wisdom. God's *wisdom* is His perfect awareness of what is happening in all of His creation in any given moment. This includes His knowledge of the final outcome of His creation and of how He will work from beginning to ending of human history (Job 11:4-12; 28:1-28; Ps. 139; Rom. 11).

Psalm 90:2 *"Before the mountains were brought forth or ever you had formed the earth and the world, even from everlasting to everlasting, you are God".*

Rev 21:1"Behold the dwelling place of God is with men". NAMES OF GOD : The name of God is a personal disclosure and reveals His relationship with His people. His name is known only because He chooses to make it known. To the Hebrew mind, God was both hidden and revealed, transcendent and immanent. Even though he was mysterious, lofty, and unapproachable, He bridged the gap with humankind by revealing His name. God's righteousness expresses itself in many ways (Ex. 2:23-25; Josh. 23:1-16; Ps. 71:14-21; Isa. 51:5-8; Acts 10:34-35; Rom. 3:5-26). He is the ultimate standard of right and wrong. He is faithful, constant, and unchanging in His character. He defends the defenseless, helpless, victimized, and oppressed. He opposes evil through personal expressions of His wrath, anger, judgment, punishment, and jealousy.

God is, simultaneously, transcendent and immanent, is supreme in His Excellence, and is independent of all experiences, such as birth and death.

All instructions and understandings are His; the mansions and sanctuaries are His, as well. Without Him, I know no other, O my Lord and Master; I continually sing His Glorious Praises. All beings and creatures seek the Protection of His Sanctuary; all thought of their care rests with Him. That which pleases His Will is good; this alone is Nanak's prayer.[795 SGGS]

He is my Father, and He is my Mother. He is my Relative, and He is my Brother. He is my Protector everywhere; why should I feel any fear or anxiety? By His Grace, I recognize Him. He is my Shelter, and He is my Honor. Without Him, there is no other; the entire Universe is the Arena of His play. He has created all beings and creatures. As it pleases Him, He assigns tasks to one and all. All Actions are His handiwork; we can do nothing, by ourselves. Meditating on His Name, I have rediscovered (after experiencing the phase of being separated, from Him) GREAT PEACE & SOLACE. Singing the Glorious Praises of the Lord, my mind is cooled and soothed. Through the Perfect Guru, congratulations are pouring in—Nanak is victorious on the arduous battlefield of life! [103 SGGS]

General Revelation The physical world—nature—is not a part of God as my hand is a part of me. Yet, God might reveal Himself through His actions in that world. Besides saying or writing things, persons may reveal facts about themselves in other ways, such as physical gestures or facial expressions. Sometimes persons' actions communicate whether they are selfish or generous, clumsy or skillful. A grimace, a smile, or a frown can often be telling. Transferring these things to a theological context is not simple, because God is not visible. He does not have facial features or bodily parts with which to gesture. To say God reveals Himself through nature means that God communicates to us things about Himself that we would otherwise not know through the events of the physical world, only, but also through physical world itself (Ps.19:1)

What sort of things might God tell us in this manner? Paul explained "What can be known about God is plain to them, for God Himself made it plain. Ever since God created the world, his invisible qualities both his eternal power and his divine nature, have been clearly seen; they are perceived in the things that God has made. So those people have no excuse at all" (Rom. 1:20 TEV). The psalmist (Ps. 19:1) saw the glory of God through the spectacles of special revelation. What the psalmist saw was objectively and genuinely there. We can rephrase these observations to say that all that can be known about God in a natural sense has been revealed in nature. This is what we call natural or general revelation. General revelation is universal in the sense that it is God's self-disclosure of Himself in a general way to all people at all times in all places. General revelation occurs through (1) nature, (2) in our experience and in our conscience, and (3) in history.

Pilgrimages, austere discipline, compassion and charity—these, by themselves, bring only an iota of merit. Listening and believing with love and humility in one's mind, one cleanses oneself with the Name, at the sacred shrine deep within. All virtues are the Lord's, humans have none at all. None has the ability to decipher the Lord's coded limits. The time of the Creation of the Universe is not known to any religious Priests, or to the Yogis. One who claims to know everything shall not be decorated in the world hereafter. [4 SGGS]

Now, to realize and to know Truth, the exact nature of Falsehood needs to be understood, in the correct perspective.

False are body, wealth, and all relations. False are ego, possessiveness and Maya (Illusion). False are power, youth, wealth and property. False are sexual desire and wild anger. False are chariots, elephants, horses and expensive clothes. False are deception, emotional attachment and egotistical pride. False is self-conceit. Only devotional worship is Permanent, Constant and TRUTH. Nanak lives by meditating, on the Lotus Feet of the Lord. False are the ears, which listen to the slander of others. False are the hands, which steal the wealth of others. False are the eyes, which gaze, stealthily, upon the beauty of another's wife. False is the tongue which enjoys delicacies and external tastes. False are the feet, which run to do evil to others. False is the mind, which covets the wealth of others. False is the body, which does not do good to others. Without understanding, everything is false. Blessed is that body, says Nanak, that remembers the Lord's Name.[268 SGGS]

The Supreme **One** is a Reality. Truth, Fact or Reality exists at two planes: Mental and Material. Mind observes the Universe through the medium of the Senses, and all that is observed is a Reality. Matter, too, is a Realistic-Entity. And, Human beings are a combination of Mind, Matter, and Spirit & Intelligence. All of these, together, constitute Truth. God, alone, is the undisputed, unchallenged Truth.

TRINITY Theological term used to define God as an undivided unity expressed in the threefold nature of God the Father, God the Son, and God the Holy Spirit. As a distinctive Christian doctrine, the Trinity is considered as a divine mystery beyond human comprehension to be reflected upon only through scriptural revelation. While the term *trinity* does not appear in Scripture, the Trinitarian structure appears throughout the New Testament to affirm that God Himself is manifested through Jesus Christ by means of the Spirit.

A proper biblical view of the Trinity balances the concepts of unity and distinctiveness. Two errors that appear in the history of the consideration of the doctrine are ditheism and Unitarianism. In tritheism, error is made in emphasizing the distinctiveness of the Godhead to the point that the Trinity is seen as three separate Gods, or a Christian polytheism. On the other hand, Unitarianism excludes the concept of distinctiveness while focusing solely on the aspect of God the Father. In this way, Christ and the Holy Spirit are placed in lower categories and made less than divine. Both errors compromise the effectiveness and contribution of the activity of God in redemptive history.

Isaiah 45:5:12 *"I made the earth and created men upon it. It was my hands that stretched out the heavens, and I command all".*

Jeremiah 32:17 *"Ah Lord God ! Behold you have made the heaven and earth by your great power".*

His word created everything. [3 SGGS]

God is the Creator of Nature. God's Grace is also part of His Nature; so:

By His Nature we see, by His Nature we hear; by His Nature we have fear, and the essence of happiness. By His Nature the nether worlds exist, and the ethereal ones; by His Nature the entire creation exists. By His Nature the Holy Scriptures of the Hindu, Jewish, Christian and Islamic religions are compiled. By His Nature all deliberations are held. By His Nature we eat, drink and dress; by His Nature all love exists. By His Nature come the species of all kinds and colors; by His Nature the living beings of the world exist. By His Nature virtues exist, and by His Nature vices exist. By His Nature come honor and dishonor. By His Nature wind, water and fire exist; by His Nature earth and dust exist. Everything is in Your Nature, Lord; He is the All-Powerful Creator. His Name is the Holiest of the Holy. Says Nanak, through the Command of His Will, He beholds and pervades the creation; He is absolutely unrivalled. [464 SGGS]

He fashioned the creation; seated within the creation, He beholds it with delight. He is the Giver and the Creator; by His Pleasure, He bestows His Mercy. He is the Knower of all; He gives life, and takes it away, again with a Single-Word (Command). Seated within the creation, He beholds it with delight. [463 SGGS]

He himself is the Creator. Everything that happens is His Doing. There is none except Him. He designed the Creations; He beholds it and He understands it. Says servant Nanak, the Lord is revealed to the aspirant-soul, who is God-loving, such a one is the Living Expression of the Guru's Word. [12 SGGS]

"Peter said to Him, 'Lord, why can I not follow You now?' " (John 13:37).

There are times when you can't understand why you cannot do what you want to do. When God brings a time of waiting, and appears to be unresponsive, don't fill it with busyness, just wait. The time of waiting may come to teach you the meaning of sanctification—to be set apart from sin and made holy—or it may come after the process of sanctification has begun to teach you what service means. Never run before God gives you His direction. If you have the slightest doubt, then He is not guiding. Whenever there is doubt—wait.

At first you may see clearly what God's will is—the severance of a friendship, the breaking off of a business relationship, or something else you feel is distinctly God's will for you to do. But never act on the impulse of that feeling. If you do, you will cause difficult situations to arise, which will take years to untangle. Wait for God's timing and He will do it without any heartache or disappointment. When it is a question of the providential will of God, wait for God to move.

Peter did not wait for God. He predicted in his own mind where the test would come, and it came where he did not expect it. "I will lay down my life for Your sake." Peter's statement was honest but ignorant. "Jesus answered him, ' ... the rooster shall not crow till you have denied me three times' " (13:38). This was said with a deeper knowledge of Peter than Peter had of himself. He could not follow Jesus because he did not know himself or his own capabilities well enough. Natural devotion may be enough to attract us to Jesus, to make us feel His irresistible charm, but it will never make us disciples. Natural devotion will deny Jesus, always falling short of what it means to truly follow Him.

You are my father and my mother . [103 SGGS]

You are the common father of all. [97 SGGS]

True is the Master, True is His Name—speak it with infinite love. People beg and pray, and the Great Giver distributes His Gifts, so very magnanimously, and in abundance. So, what offering can we place before Him, by which we might have an Exclusive Audience, with HIM? What words can we speak to evoke His Love? In the ambrosial hours before dawn, chant the True Name, and contemplate upon His Glorious Greatness. By the karma of past actions, the magnificently exquisite robe (this physical body) is obtained. By His Grace, the Gate of Liberation is found. Know this well: the True One Himself is All. [2 SGGS]

His Blessings are so abundant that there can be no written account of them. The Great Giver does not hold back anything. There are so many great, heroic warriors begging at the Door of the Infinite Lord. So many creations contemplate and dwell upon Him, that they cannot be counted. So many perish, engaged in corruption. So many enjoy HIS Bounties, and then deny receiving. So many foolish consumers keep on consuming. So many endure distress, deprivation and constant abuse. Even these are Your Gifts, O Great Giver! Liberation from bondage comes only by Your Will. No one else has any say. If some fool should presume that he does have a say, he shall learn, and feel the effects of his folly. He Himself knows, He Himself gives. Few, and rarest of the rare are those who acknowledge this.[5 SGGS]

"I heard the voice of the Lord, saying: 'Whom shall I send, and who will go for us?' " (Isaiah 6:8).

When we talk about the call of God, we often forget the most important thing, namely, the nature of Him who calls. There are many things calling each of us today. Some of these calls will be answered, and others will not even be heard. The call is the expression of the nature of the One who calls, and we can only recognize the call if that same nature is in us. The call of God is the expression of God's nature, not ours. God providentially weaves the threads of His call through our lives, and only we can distinguish them. It is the threading of God's voice directly to us over a certain concern; yet, sometimes, it helps to seek another person's opinion of it. Our dealings over the call of God should be kept exclusively between Him and ourselves.

The call of God is a reflection of my nature, just as my personal desires and temperament are of some consideration. As long as I dwell on my own qualities and traits and think about what I am suited for, I will never hear the call of God. But when God brings me into the right relationship with Himself, I will be in the same condition Isaiah was. Isaiah was so attuned to God, because of the great crisis he had just endured, that the call of God penetrated his soul. The majority of us cannot hear anything but ourselves. And we cannot hear anything God says. But to be brought to the place where we can hear the call of God is to be profoundly changed. The call is never a "once-and-for-all-time" event. God continues His call and shapes us along the way (Abraham episode in Gen. 12).

All happiness comes, when God is pleased. The Feet of the Perfect Guru dwell in the mind. Become intuitively absorbed in introspective meditation. My Lord, the Master is Inaccessible and Unfathomable. Deep within each and every heart, He dwells near and close at hand. He is always detached; How rare is that person who understands his own self. This is the sign of Communion with God: in the mind, the Command of the True Lord is recognized. Intuitive peace and poise, contentment, enduring satisfaction and bliss come through the Pleasure of the Master's Will. God, the Great Giver, has given me His Hand. He has eliminated all sickness and misery, all doubt and penury, all pain and fear, of birth and death. Says Nanak, those whom God has made His Chosen-ones, rejoice in the pleasure of singing the Hymns of the Lord's Praises.[106 SGGS]

This, then, is the Life-Divine. And, it is made available, to only a select and chosen few, by the Lord, who showers all the bounties at His disposal, on his devotees.

Genesis 5-7

"And God saw that the wickedness of man was great on the earth, and that every imagination of the thoughts of his heart was only evil continually.

And it repented the Lord that He had made man on the earth, and it grieved Him at His heart.

And the Lord said: I will destroy man whom I have created from the face of the earth; both man and beast, and the creeping thing, and the fowls of the air; for it repenteth me that I have made them".

Everyone makes mistakes, but God and His messengers are infallible.
[60 SGGS]

Do not blame the Sovereign Lord; when someone grows old, his
intellect leaves him. The blind man talks and babbles, and then falls
into the ditch. All that the Perfect Lord does is perfect; there is not too
little, or too much. Says Nanak, the God-loving Person merges into the
Perfect Lord. [1412 SGGS]
(Do not become like the infirm or the blind, while you have all
faculties, intact, to reason out issues).

This Unison & Harmonious Blend, between God & Man, is termed
communion. In such a state, one does not criticize God's decisions and
refrains from denying His existence.

The Supreme Lord, the Transcendent Lord, the True Guru, saves all.
Hence, it is unbecoming to criticize God's decisions, his ways and his
works. Says Nanak, without the Guru, no one crosses over the
turbulent life-ocean; this is the perfect essence
of all contemplation.[611 SGGS]

FINGER OF GOD A picturesque expression of God at work. The finger of God writing the Ten Commandments illustrated God's giving the law without any mediation (Ex. 31:18; Deut. 9:10). Elsewhere the finger of God suggests God's power to bring plagues on Egypt (Ex. 8:19) and in making the heavens (Ps. 8:3). Jesus' statement "If I with the finger of God cast out devils, no doubt the kingdom of God is come upon you" (Luke 11:20) means that since Jesus cast out demons by the power of God, God's rule had become a reality among His hearers.

Limitations of Satan Today, people continue to concretize their fears. They want a scapegoat to deliver them from responsibility. Satan is a created, rebellious and tempting evil power active in the universe, but his powerful existence does not exclude a person from responsibility. Satan and the demonic forces cannot dominate or possess us except by our own consent. Believers will not be tempted beyond our power of resistance (1 Cor. 10:13). The power of Satan is limited. He acts within the limits set by divine sovereignty. The believer has God's armor—the biblical gospel, integrity, peace through Christ, faith in Christ, prayer—as spiritual security (Eph. 6:11-18).

The recent fascination with Satan and demons is in reaction to an earlier disbelief. Christians should beware of excessive gullibility as well as extreme oversimplification. Knowledge about Satan and evil angels alerts Christians to the danger and subtlety of satanic temptation. We should not become too absorbed in satanic forces. Satan and demonic forces are active, but they are limited.

All creations reside within His mind; He watches and moves them under His Graceful glance. The Lord grants them glory, and Himself causes them to act. The Lord is the greatest of the great; great is His world. He assigns them their tasks. If He should cast an angry glance, He could transform Kings into gardeners. Even though they may beg from door to door, no one will give them charity.[472 SGGS]

On the contrary, God, during His pleasure, may grant the boon of a Kingdom, to a penniless devotee, who is Truth-Incarnate.

None can comprehend the confines of His Royal-Abode, neither does anyone have the requisite faculties to understand Your Powers. One who goes laughing, returns crying, and the one who goes crying returns laughing. What is inhabited becomes deserted, and what is deserted becomes inhabited. And, all of it happens by His Decree. The rivers dry out, into a desert, the desert turns into a well, and the well turns into a mountain, and mountains crumble under their own weight. From the earth, the mortal is exalted to the Ethereal-Worlds (realms); and from the ethers on high, he plunges down. The beggar is transformed into a king, and the king into a pauper. The idiotic fool is transformed into a Pandit, a religious scholar, and the Pandit into a fool. The woman is transformed into a man, and the man into woman. Says Kabeer : God is the Beloved of the Holy Saints. [1252 SGGS]

Tigers, hawks, falcons and eagles—the Lord could make them eat grass. And those animals which eat grass—He could make them eat meat. He could radically alter anyone's life. He could raise dry land from the rivers, and turn the deserts into bottomless oceans. He could anoint a measly worm as a king, and reduce an army to ashes. All beings and creatures live by breathing, but He could keep us alive, even without the breath. Says Nanak : As it pleases the True Lord, He sustains all. [144 SGGS]

The relation of the cross to forgiveness of sins was implicit in the earliest Christian preaching (Acts 2:21; 3:6, 19; 4:13; 5:31; 8:35; 10:43). Also, in prophetic literature (Isa. 53:6). Paul proclaimed that "Christ died for our sins"(1 Cor. 15:3), that He was a "propitiation" (Rom. 3:25 KJV; "sacrifice of atonement," NRSV, NIV; "expiation," RSV), that He became "a curse for us" (Gal. 3:13), and that those "who sometimes were far off are made nigh by the blood of Christ" (Eph. 2:13). Furthermore, "Christ was once offered to bear the sins of many" (Heb. 9:28) and has become "a new and living way" (Heb. 10:20) into God's presence. He is the one who "bare our sins in his own body on the tree" (1 Pet. 2:24).

Christ may be understood by this saying to mean, that a clear and abundant revelation of God's will should be now made unto men; that heaven itself should be laid as it were open, and all the mysteries which had been shut up and hidden in it from eternity, relative to the salvation and glorification of man; should be now fully revealed. The payment for the penalty of sin is fully, and only, available because of the sacrifice of Jesus.

Rejoice in the Lord always—Be continually happy; but this happiness you can find only in the Lord. Genuine happiness is spiritual; as it can only come from God, so it infallibly tends to him. The apostle repeats the exhortation, to show, not only his earnestness, but also that it was God's will that it should be so, and that it was their duty as well as interest.

Matthew 18:14 It is not the will of your Father—If any soul be finally lost, it is not because God's will or counsel was against its salvation, or that a proper provision had not been made for it; but that, though light came into the world, it preferred darkness to light, because of its attachment to its evil deeds.

He wills and creates everything. [292 SGGS]

Those who take pleasure in God's Will, doubt shall be eliminated from within them. Know Him as the True Guru, who unites all with the Lord. Meeting with the True Guru, they receive the fruits of their destiny, and egotism is driven out from within. The pain of evil-mindedness is eliminated; good fortune radiates on their foreheads.[72 SGGS]

Sayeth Sheikh Farid, a Muslim Seer : *Treat Sorrow and Happiness, as the same par value, and conquer the vices, and banish them from your heart and soul, forever. God appreciates such people and they are honored in HIS court.[1383 SGGS]*

One who obeys His Will, becomes the recipient of His Gracious Vision. That alone is devotional worship, which is pleasing to His Will. He is the Nourisher of all beings. The Sovereign Lord is the Support of the Saints. Whatever pleases Him, they accept. He is the sustenance of their minds and bodies.[747 SGGS]

Naked we come, and naked we go. This is by the Lord's Command; what else can we do? All objects belong to Him; He shall take them away (life and death are under His Will). One who loves Him, accepts God's Will; he intuitively drinks in the Lord's sublime-essence. Says Nanak : Praise the Giver of peace, forever; chant and savor the Lord's Name, always.[1246 SGGS]

Meditate, continually and constantly, on the Name of the Lord within your heart. Thus shall one rescue all companions and associates, along with oneself. The Guru is always with such a disciple, near at hand. Meditating, and reminiscing about Him, cherish Him forever. Nanak begs for the treasure of the Name of the Lord. [394 SGGS]

Section 2

Change YOUR Life

****

Let's concentrate on the wondrous
SIMILARITIES
instead of harping on the differences,
in order that we may, all
serve humanity, in unison and tandem.

The
GREATEST
Commonality is that all of us are
HIS CREATIONS.

Jesus commands that wherever there are two or more, enjoined in collective prayer, there God resideth.

Answered Prayers—Unanswered Petitions Not every petition is granted. Job's demand for answers from God was eclipsed by the awesome privilege of encountering Him (Job 38-41). Modern believers must also cherish communion with the Father more than their petitions.

Jesus, with His soul sorrowful to the point of death, prayed three times that His cup of suffering might pass, but He was nevertheless submissive to God's will (Matt. 26:38-39, 42, 45). Both the boldness of the petition to alter God's will and the submission to this "hard" path of suffering are significant.

Paul asked three times for deliverance from his "thorn in the flesh." God's answer to Paul directed him to find comfort in God's sufficient grace. Also God declared that His power is best seen in Paul's weakness (2 Cor. 12:8-9). God gave him the problem to hinder his pride. Ironically, Paul claimed that God gave the problem, and yet he called it a messenger of Satan. Paul learned that petitions are sometimes denied in light of an eventual greater good: God's power displayed in Paul's humility.

Faith is a condition for answered petitions (Mark 11:24). Two extremes must be avoided concerning faith. (1) With Jesus' example in mind we must not think that faith will always cause our wishes to be granted. (2) Also we must not go through the motions of prayer without faith. Believers do not receive what they pray for because they pray from selfish motives (Jas. 4:2-3). Prayers are also hindered by corrupted character (Jas. 4:7) or injured relationships (Matt. 5:23-24). (4) Whatever we ask, has to be in the name of Jesus, because of who he is, and what he has done, we can know that God hears our prayers.

The Creator resides in the Holy Congregation [153 SGGS].
All afflictions visit one who forgets the Lord. [135 SGGS]
Praying for anything other than Your Grace, O' Lord, leads me from
one problem to another. Bless me that the hunger in my mind is
quenched, once and for all.[958 SGGS]
The Merciful Creator grabs hold of the mortal's arm, and pulls him
up and out of misery. Joining the Holy Congregation, the mortal's
bonds are broken, and the Guru redeems him.[1141 SGGS].

The 3 pillars of the Rock-like steadfast "Monument of Prayer" are:
Service, Meditation, and Total Surrender of one's Ego.
God confers solace and fearlessness. Prayer is an essential ingredient
of the "Faith-in-God" Doctrine, which emphasizes that God is, always,
right. ***Doubt should not be permitted to creep in, on this count.***
Hence, one must pray to God, the Source and the Light, at all times,
day or night, in joy or sorrow, and on all significant occasions, like
birth, naming-ceremony, wedding, death, commencement of
educational or business ventures. PRAY to God, at all times, in
prosperity or adversity. The concept of Prayer is engrained in the Sikh
Psyche and Belief-Structure. It says that God is not a Law of Nature,
alone, nor of Karma, or of Pre-Determination, alone. It is, in essence,
all of these, together, and even much more.   HIS Grace can
modify/amend the Negative-Writ, to rescue the bereaved one, who is,
now, praying and wailing, in agony, for help. The Savior is
Omnipresent and All Pervasive. Hence, we see that God is
Transcendental and Immanent, both, at once. After crossing the
Barriers, Hindrances and Obstacles of Physical Desires, Material
Gains and Mental Traumas, one is forced to (there's no alternative
available, there's no other strategy to be employed) pray to the Lord,
for express grant of Sublime and Pristine Grace. This, then, is the
finality of spiritual elevation. Prayer, when coupled with sincere
Meditative-Contemplation, becomes an extremely potent force, that
could radically alter the prevailing scenario, thereby bringing about a
positive transformation, in the life of the devotee. The deity is in the
heart and soul, and is not to be searched, anywhere else.

Healing could be done at various plains : Physical, emotional, psychological, and spiritual. Sin is the greatest of all diseases; it's the ultimate 'sickness'. It eats at the core of the soul, and has a spilling effect on all the aforesaid levels, as also on mental, social and moral plains.

From what we seek to be healed is the moot question?
Luke 8:42 "His only child was dying, a little girl of twelve".

Mark 1:40 "A man with leprosy came and knelt before Jesus, begging to be healed".
Isaiah 61:1 "He has sent me to comfort the broken-hearted. Our broken hearts need healing and restoration".
Psalm 30:1 "You have turned my mourning into joyful dancing".
Psalm 55:20 "we need healing from the pain of betrayal".
Romans 6:23 "For, the wage of sin is death, but the great gift of God is eternal life".
Psalm 103:3-4 "He forgives all my sins".
How does God heal?
2 Kings 20:7 "Make an ointment from figs and spread it over the boil". They did this and Hezekiah recovered.
Psalm 119:93 "I will never forget your commandments, for you have used them to restore my joy and health".
Isaih 38:16 "Lord, your discipline is good, for it leads to life and health".

Promises from God:

Psalm 147:3 "God heals the broken-hearted".
Malachi 4:2 "god will heal us and restore us".
It must be borne in mind, though, that it is not, always, God's Will to heal (2 Cor. 12:7-9).

One is blessed with peace, pleasure, bliss, and the celestial sound current, gazing upon the feet of God. The Savior has saved him, and the True Guru has cured the fever of his mind. He has been rescued, in the True Guru's Sanctuary; service to Him does not go in vain".(619 SGGS)

"All sufferings have come to an end, and all diseases have been eradicated. God has showered His Grace. Twenty-four hours a day, worship and adore the Lord and Master; all efforts have come to fruition. O Dear Lord, You are my peace, wealth and capital. Please, save me, O my Beloved! I offer this prayer to my God. Whatever I ask for, I receive; I have total faith in my Master. Says Nanak, I have met with the Perfect Guru, and all my fears have been dispelled". (619 SGGS)

The Destroyer of sorrow is God's Name; Twenty-four hours a day, dwell upon the wisdom of the Perfect True Guru. That heart, in which the Supreme Lord God abides, is the most beautiful place. The Messenger of Death does not even approach those who chant the Glorious Praises of the Lord with the tongue. When the Lord of the Universe becomes merciful, sorrow and suffering departed. The hot winds do not even touch those who are protected by the True Guru. The Guru is the True Creator Lord. When the Guru was totally satisfied, I obtained everything. (218 SGGS)

The Creator has brought utter peace to the aspirant's home; misery has left his family. The Perfect Guru has saved him. He who sought the Sanctuary of the True Lord is saved. The Transcendent Lord Himself has become his Protector. Tranquility, intuitive peace and poise welled up in an instant, and his mind was comforted forever. The Lord gave him the edicine of His Name, which has cured all misery. God extended His Mercy to the devotee, and resolved all his matters. God confirmed His loving nature; He did not take the aspirant's merits or demerits into account. (622 SGGS)

Colossians, Epistle to the Ephesians : Was written by Paul at Rome during his first imprisonment there (Acts 28:16, 30), probably in the spring of A.D. 57, or, as some think, 62, and soon after he had written his Epistle to the Ephesians. Like some of his other epistles (e.g., those to Corinth), this seems to have been written in consequence of information which had somehow been conveyed to him of the internal state of the church there (Col. 1:4-8). Its object was to counteract false teaching. A large part of it is directed against certain speculatists who attempted to combine the doctrines of Oriental mysticism and asceticism with Christianity, thereby promising the disciples the enjoyment of a higher spiritual life and a deeper insight into the world of spirits. Paul argues against such teaching, showing that in Christ Jesus they had all things. He sets forth the majesty of his redemption. The mention of the "new moon" and "Sabbath days" (Col. 2:16) shows also that there were here Judaizing teachers who sought to draw away the disciples from the simplicity of the gospel.

Like most of Paul's epistles, this consists of two parts, a doctrinal and a practical. (1) The doctrinal part comprises the first two chapters. His main theme is developed in chapter 2. He warns them against being drawn away from Him in whom dwelt all the fullness of the Godhead, and who was the head of all spiritual powers. Christ was the head of the body of which they were members; and if they were truly united to him, what needed they more?   (2.) The practical part of the epistle (Col. 3-4) enforces various duties naturally flowing from the doctrines expounded. They are exhorted to mind things that are above (Col. 3:1-4), to mortify every evil principle of their nature, and to put on the new man (Col. 3:5-14).

Endless are His Praises, endless are those who speak them. Endless are His Actions, endless are His Gifts. Endless is His Vision, endless is His Hearing. What is the Mystery of His Mind? Its limits here and beyond cannot be perceived. HE is incomprehensible. The more one talks about HIS limits, infinitely more there still remains to be said. Great is the Master, High is His Heavenly Home. Highest of the High, above all is His Name. Only one as Great and as High as God can know His Lofty and Exalted State. Only He Himself is that Great. He Himself knows Himself. Reassures Nanak : by His Gracious Glance, He bestows His Benediction.[5 SGGS]

The negative feeling of Life-Negation should not, and must not, be given any leverage, whatsoever. One must strive to lead a worthy life in all respects : Work for subsistence & sustenance, pray and meditate for spiritual-elevation, bear an exemplary moral character, abiding by the Code of Ethics (relating to adultery, fraudulent practices, oppression & tyranny, helping the deserving and needy), and never to renounce the world to become a reclusive-entity (thereby becoming a burden on the society).

Great emphasis has been laid on virtue & morality, as against the hitherto prevalent stress on The Law of KARMA, alone, according to which : " Worthy deeds shall bear good and tasty fruits (respect, glory, health & prosperity), while evil deeds shall bring forth or reap misery/pain, in the form and shape of disease, poverty, and the Victory-of-Vice, in general. An amalgamation of VIRTUE and KARMA (Deed /Action) is advocated. The world is not an illusionary concept: It is a reality.

True are His worlds, True are His solar Systems. True are His realms, True is His Creation. True are His actions, and all His deliberations. True is His Command, and True is His Court. True is the Command of His Will, True is His Decree.[463 SGGS]

CREATION From ancient times persons have had a keen interest in the origin of the universe. Stories or fragments of stories about creation have survived in the literature of several ancient nations. Biblical writers may reflect an awareness of these extra-biblical accounts, but their consistent testimony is that Israel's God was the Creator. His creative activities proceeded in orderly and methodical fashion toward the fulfillment of His purpose to create "good heavens" and "a good earth."

Biblical References to Creation Probably the best-known reference to creation in the Bible is Genesis 1:1-2:4a. That certainly is not the only place in Scripture where the subject is treated. Psalmists mentioned creation or the Creator frequently (Pss. 8:3, 4; 74:17; 95:5; 100:3; 104:24, 30; 118:24; 40:5; 51:10; 64:9; 24:1-2; 102:25; 145:10). The second half of Isaiah (chs. 40-66) has four direct references to creation (Isa. 40:28; 43:7, 15; 45:7; 65:17). Job alluded to creation in two speeches (Job 10:8; 26:7), and God's answer to Job contains one reference to the subject (Job 38:4).

The New Testament reveals that Jesus "made" all things (John 1:3) and that "all things were created by him, and for him" (Col. 1:16). Paul's assertion recorded in Ephesians 3:9 is that God "created all things." The writer of Hebrews notes that Jesus was the agent God used to create the world (Heb. 1:2). Because God created all things, He is worthy of "glory and honor and power" (Rev. 4:11). Luke testified that the living God "made heaven, and earth, and the sea, and all things that are therein" (Acts 14:15). The consistent report of the Bible is that God is the Source of the whole created order.

There are several galaxies and constellations God created; many earths like the one we live upon; many stars, moons, suns, and other such bodies. [275 SGGS]

In the Primal Void, the Infinite Lord assumed His Power. He Himself is unattached, infinite and incomparable. He created the universe, and the fortress-like body. His Light pervades fire, water and souls; His Power rests in the Primal Void From this Primal Void, came the moon, the sun and the earth. His Light pervades all the three worlds. The Lord of this Primal Void is unseen, infinite and immaculate; He is absorbed in the Primal Trance of Deep Meditation. From this Primal Void, the earth and the Ethers were created. He made both night and day; creation and destruction, pleasure and pain. The God-loving person is immortal, untouched by pleasure and pain. None of the Scriptures can describe His worth. We speak as He inspires us to speak. From the Primal Void, He created the seven nether regions. From the Primal Void, He established this world to lovingly dwell upon Him. The Infinite Lord Himself created the creation. Everyone acts as He makes them act, Lord. His Power is diffused through the deficiencies and vices, or the positive qualities. Through egotism, they suffer the pains of birth and death. Those blessed by His Grace become God-loving people; they attain the fourth state of Redemption. From the Primal Void, all the incarnations welled up. He made the expanse. He fashioned the demi-gods and demons, the heavenly heralds and celestial musicians; everyone acts according to their past karma. The True Guru, like the Primal Being, is sublime and detached. Attuned to the Word of the Holy hymns, he is intoxicated with the sublime essence of the Lord. Riches, intellect, miraculous spiritual powers and spiritual wisdom are obtained from the Guru; through perfect destiny, they are received. This mind is madly obsessed with Illusion. Only a few are spiritually wise enough to understand and know this. Proclaims Nanak : the immaculate resonance of the Celestial music, and the Music of the Holy hymns resound; and thus one merges into the True Name of the Lord. [1037 SGGS]

64

Moses seemed unwilling to leave his work; but that being finished, he manifested no unwillingness to die. God had declared that he should not enter Canaan. But the Lord also promised that Moses should have a view of it, and showed him all that good land. Such a sight believers now have, through grace, of the bliss and glory of their future state. Sometimes God reserves the brightest discoveries of his grace to his people to support their dying moments. Those may leave this world with cheerfulness, who die in the faith of Christ, and in the hope of heaven.

In the bunch of unripe grapes, at present of no value, the new wine is contained. The Jews have been kept a distinct people, that all may witness the fulfillment of ancient prophesies and promises. God's chosen, the spiritual seed of praying Jacob, shall inherit his mountains of bliss and joy, and be carried safe to them through the vale of tears. All things are for the display of God's glory in the redemption of sinners.

Let young persons set out in life with learning the fear of the Lord, if they desire true comfort here, and eternal happiness hereafter. Those will be most happy who begin the soonest to serve so good a Master. All aim to be happy. Surely they must look further than the present world, for man's life on earth consists but of few days, and those full of trouble. What man is he that would see the good of that where all bliss is perfect? Alas! Few have this good in their thoughts. That religion promises best, which creates watchfulness over the heart and over the tongue. We can fix the hour and minute of the sun's rising and setting tomorrow, but we cannot fix the certain time of a vapor being scattered. So short, unreal, and fading is human life, and all the prosperity or enjoyment that attends it, though bliss or woe forever must be according to our conduct during the fleeting moment.

With whom does one share this ecstatic feeling of peace and bliss, while gazing upon the Blessed Vision of God's Audience.   Drinking the Invaluable Nectar of the Name of the Lord, one relishes its taste. Like the mute, one can only smile — but cannot speak of its flavor. As the breath is held in bondage, none can understand the cause of its inhalation and exhalation.   So is that person, whose heart is enlightened by the Lord — his story cannot be told. The Absolute, Formless, Eternally Unchanging, Unfathomable Lord cannot be measured. Says Nanak, whoever endures the unendurable — this state belongs to him alone.[1205 SGGS]

Inner peace in a person, draws others to that person, like a magnetic force; there's an aura of power attached to this sense of peace and joy. The environs become surcharged with positive energy, and it gets transmitted, automatically, to those who come into close proximity of that person. The highest forces of the power of divinity and nature become one's natural allies, so to say, in thwarting challenges, obstacles, and warding off dangers, hallucinations, illusions, and superstitions.

*Baygumpura, 'the city without sorrow', is the name of the town. There is no suffering or anxiety there. There are no troubles or taxes on commodities there. There is no fear, blemish or downfall there. Now, having discovered this excellent city, the aspirant finds there is ever-lasting peace and safety there, O Siblings of Destiny.   God's Kingdom is steady, stable and eternal. There is no second or third status; all are equal there. That city is populous and eternally famous. Those who live there are wealthy and contented.   They stroll about freely, just as they please. They know the Mansion of the Lord's Presence, and none dares block their path, or create impediments. [345 SGGS]
*This town is located in our hearts, our souls; we do not need to go anywhere, as God resides within us. Searching our inner-self, we are sure to find God, always guiding us, looking over us.

"I have appeared to you for this purpose ..." (Acts 26:16).

The vision Paul had on the road to Damascus was not a passing emotional experience, but a vision that had very clear and emphatic directions for him. And Paul stated, "I was not disobedient to the heavenly vision" (Acts 26:19). Our Lord said to Paul, in effect, "Your whole life is to be overpowered or subdued by me; you are to have no end, no aim, and no purpose but Mine." And the Lord also says to us, "You did not choose me, but *I chose you* and appointed you that you should go ..." (John 15:16).

When we are born again, our hearts and minds undergo a change; if we are spiritual at all, we have visions of what Jesus wants us to be. It is important that I learn not to be "disobedient to the heavenly vision"— not to doubt that it can be attained. It is not enough to give mental assent to the fact that God has redeemed the world, or even to know that the Holy Spirit can make all that Jesus did a reality in my life. I must have the foundation of a personal relationship with Him. Paul was not given a message or a doctrine to proclaim. He was brought into a vivid, personal, overpowering relationship with Jesus Christ. Acts 26:16 are tremendously compelling "... to make you a minister and a witness." There would be nothing there without a personal relationship. Paul was devoted to a Person, not to a cause. He was absolutely Jesus Christ's. He saw nothing else and he lived for nothing else. "For I determined not to know anything among you except Jesus Christ and Him crucified" (1 Corinthians 2:2).

O man you were sent here to gain merit, but you are engrossed in futile activities, and your time is running out. [43 SGGS]

First, the baby loves mother's milk; second, he learns of his mother and father; third, his brothers, sisters and aunts; fourth, the love of play awakens. Fifth, he runs after food and drink; sixth, in his sexual desire, he does not respect social customs. Seventh, he gathers wealth and dwells in his house; eighth, he becomes angry, and his body is consumed. Ninth, he turns gray, and his breathing becomes labored; tenth, he is cremated, and turns to ashes. His companions send him off, crying out and lamenting. The swan of the soul takes flight, and asks which way to go. He came and he went, and now, even his name has died. O Nanak, the self-willed egoistic persons love the darkness. Without the Guru, the world is drowning. 137 SGGS]

The ideals or purposes, of life, undergo a rapid transformation, in consonance with the change and variance in socio-economic and polito- religious environment & conditions, cultural background, levels of education /literacy, God-gifted talents & intelligence, and of course, with advancing age. Hence, it can be safely inferred and assumed that the purpose-of-life, for an infant, would, surely, differ from that of an adult, or of an aged-person. Priorities shift, automatically, in accordance with the change in scenario. Another significant determining factor is that the human-species has come of age, after millions of years of evolvement, commencing the journey from the most primitive of the creations of the Lord-Almighty. Advances achieved by humans are really commendable, but, in the process, God and spirituality have been relegated to the back seat, with an increasing interest in materialistic values, and pleasures of the senses, which are momentary (sexual-promiscuity, addictions, an insatiable lust and appetite for wealth and power, even at the cost of the annihilating life, on earth.

LIBERATION / EMANCIPATION / BEATITUDE

"May the God of peace Himself sanctify you completely ..." (1 Thessalonians 5:23). When we pray, asking God to sanctify us, are we prepared to measure up to what that really means? We take the word *sanctification* much too lightly. Are we prepared to pay the cost of sanctification? The cost will be a deep restriction of all our earthly concerns, and an extensive cultivation of all our godly concerns. Sanctification means to be intensely focused on God's point of view. It means to secure and to keep all the strength of our body, soul, and spirit for God's purpose alone. Are we really prepared for God to perform in us everything for which He separated us? And after He has done His work, are we then prepared to separate ourselves to God just as Jesus did? "For their sakes I sanctify myself ..." (John 17:19). The reason some of us have not entered into the experience of sanctification is that we have not realized the meaning of sanctification from God's perspective. Sanctification means being made one with Jesus so that the nature that controlled Him will control us. Are we really prepared for what that will cost? It will cost absolutely everything in us, which is not of God.

Are we prepared to be caught up into the full meaning of Paul's prayer in this verse? Are we prepared to say, "Lord, make me, a sinner saved by grace, as holy as You can"? Jesus prayed that we might be one with Him, just as He is one with the Father (see John 17:21–23). The resounding evidence of the Holy Spirit in a person's life is the unmistakable family likeness to Jesus Christ, and the freedom from everything, which is not like Him. Are we prepared to set ourselves apart for the Holy Spirit's work in us? Yet, it is in God's Hands to set us apart.

LIBERATION/ EMANCIPATION / BEATITUDE

One who, in his soul, loves the Will of God, is said to be liberated while yet alive. As is joy, so is sorrow to him. He experiences eternal bliss, and is not separated from God. As is gold, so is dust to him. As is ambrosial nectar, so is bitter poison to him. As is honor, so is dishonor. Such a one treats a pauper and a king alike. Whatever God ordains, is acceptable to such a person.[275 SGGS]
The soul-bride is in love with her Husband Lord; she focuses her consciousness on the Word of the Guru's Holy hymns. The soul-bride is joyously embellished with the gift of intuition; her hunger and thirst are taken away.[993 SGGS]

Great emphasis has been laid upon the Doctrine of "Attunement-with-God" (entering into the realm of God-consciousness). This belief relates to the Transmigration of the Soul, and Salvation, thence, would mean Total Release from the vicious cycle of birth and death. Salvation could be attained, even in the present lifetime, here and now, on our very own planet, instead of the imaginary Heavens, after death. It is very much possible that such an ecstatic level or plane is arrived at, but the only condition is that utmost restraint is required to be exercised, over the reins of the wild -horses of the senses. "PARAMPAD" (the 4th and highest state of the mind) is, in effect, the quintessential "SALVATION". The lower three states are : the Waking-state, the Dream-state, and the Dreamless-sleeping-state. Salvation means Loving God, with all the intensity & faith, at one's disposal, so as to arrive in the fragrantly wonderful zone of "Communion with God". Grace & Benediction & Benevolence play a far significant role, than Karma alone, towards the realization of this objective. Emancipation is very much possible right here, provided the pleader is sincere in his prayer and approach, and inclination and motives.

Prayerful Inner-searching "May your whole spirit, soul, and body be preserved blameless ..." (1 Thessalonians 5:23).

Your whole spirit ... ." The great, mysterious work of the Holy Spirit is in the deep recesses of our being which we cannot reach. Read Psalm 139. The psalmist implies—"O Lord, You are the God of the early mornings, the God of the late nights, the God of the mountain peaks, and the God of the sea. But, my God, my soul has horizons further away than those of early mornings, deeper darkness than the nights of earth, higher peaks than any mountain peaks, greater depths than any sea in nature. You who are the God of all these, be my God. I cannot reach to the heights or to the depths; there are motives I cannot discover, dreams I cannot realize. My God, search me."

Do we believe that God can fortify and protect our thought processes far beyond where we can go? "... the blood of Jesus Christ His Son cleanses us from all sin" (1 John 1:7). If this verse means cleansing only on our conscious level, may God have mercy on us. The man who has been dulled by sin will say that he is not even conscious of it. But the cleansing from sin we experience will reach to the heights and depths of our spirit if we will "walk in the light as He is in the light" (1:7). The same Spirit that fed the life of Jesus Christ will feed the life of our spirit. It is only when we are protected by God with the miraculous sacredness of the Holy Spirit that our spirit, soul, and body can be preserved in pure uprightness until the coming of Jesus—no longer condemned in God's sight.

We should more frequently allow our minds to meditate on these great, massive truths of God.

When the hands and the feet and the body are dirty, water can wash away the dirt. When the clothes are soiled and stained, soap can wash them clean. But when the intellect is stained and polluted by sin, it can only be cleansed by the Love of the Name. Virtue and vice do not come by mere words; actions repeated, over and over again, are engraved on the soul. One is bound to harvest what one sows. Says Nanak, by God's Command, we come and go in reincarnation.[4 SGGS]

When the mind is filthy, everything is filthy; by washing the body, the mind is not cleansed. This world is deluded by doubt; hardly anyone understands this. O' mind, chant the One Name. The True Guru has given this treasure. Even if one learns the Yogic postures of the Siddhas, and holds his sexual energy in check, still, the filth of the mind is not removed, and the filth of egotism is not eliminated. This mind is not controlled by any other discipline, except the Sanctuary of the True Guru. Meeting the True Guru, one is transformed beyond description. Prays Nanak, one who dies upon meeting the True Guru, shall be rejuvenated through the Word of the Guru's Shabad. The filth of attachment and possessiveness shall depart, and the mind shall become pure. [558 SGGS]

Like nobody prefers to sit in close proximity to a person wearing unwashed clothes, similarly a person with a 'sullied' thought-process is shunned by all and sundry, for he would only be spreading vitriolic words around, thereby vitiating the environment.

God blesses us in every sphere of life, and by meditating upon His Name, our sagging spirits are rejuvenated, and we are saved. In the Company of the Holy, filth is washed away. The Supreme Lord becomes our companion and benefactor. Continuing to meditate, the Primal-Being is sure to become the Protector, everywhere and for all times to come.

Hospitality is considered a good deed. To entertain or receive a stranger (sojourner) into one's home as an honored guest and to provide the guest with food, shelter, and protection. This was not merely an oriental custom or good manners but a sacred duty that everyone was expected to observe. Only the depraved would violate this obligation.

But, there are innumerable other worthy deeds that win God's favor. The doing of a good deed, in itself and of itself, is really insufficient and insignificant, it is the deed that is done in Faith that eventually finds favor with God.

Hospitality probably grew out of the needs of nomadic life. Since public inns were rare, a traveler had to depend on the kindness of others and had a right to expect it. This practice was extended to every sojourner, even a runaway slave (Deut. 23:16-17) or one's archenemy.

Hospitality was regarded as a sacred obligation by the ancient Greeks and Romans, one that was approved by Zeus, the god and protector of strangers. The Egyptians claimed it as a meritorious deed in life. For the Bedouins, it was an expression of righteousness. The word is not used in the Old Testament, but its elements are recognizable: Abraham and the three visitors (Gen. 18:1-8), Lot and the two angels (Gen. 19:1-8), Abraham's servant at Nahor (Gen. 24:17-33), Reuel and Moses (Ex. 2:20), Manoah and the angel (Judg. 13:15), Elijah and the widow of Zarephath (1 Kings 17:10-11), and Elisha and the Shunammite woman (2 Kings 4:8-11).

Brother, understand the Lord's sense of justice: as one sows, so does one reap. [308 SGGS]

Nobody is to be blamed, except one's own actions. Whatever misdeed one performed, for that one has suffered; so, do not blame anyone else. [433 SGGS]

ALL creatures are under the Supreme Command. According to His Will, He commands them. His Pen writes out the account of everyone.[1241 SGGS]

God driveth according to His Will; The present-life circumstances/conditions, that one finds oneself embroiled in, may be attributable to, and traceable to, the innumerable acts of commission and omission, during the past life/lives. These may be construed to be in the form and shape of rewards, or penalties, as the case may be. Virtuous deeds, in this lifetime, have the potential of presenting a human being with the invaluably cherished gift, of being spared the agony and ignominy of undergoing Transmigration.

The deluded ones have forsaken God the Primal Being, the Life of the World, and they have come to rely upon mere mortals. In the love of duality, the soul-bride is ruined; around her neck she wears the noose of Death. As one sows, so shall one harvest; your destiny is recorded on your forehead.[134 SGGS]
Fareed, the farmer plants acacia trees, and desires grapes !! He is spinning wool, but he wishes to wear silk !! [1379 SGGS]

Worthy Deeds (performed on the physical-plane) that are visible to the human-eye, are appreciated and recognized by God, in the form of worldly prestige and honor, that is, also apparent and obvious, to everyone. And, honourable Deeds, on the spiritual-plane (that cannot be viewed, even under the most advanced microscope, shall be credited to the account of the pious soul, who shall become the deserving recipient of magnificent accolades and encomiums, in the world, hereafter.

"I will very gladly spend and be spent for your souls ..." (2 Corinthians 12:15).

Once "the love of God has been poured out in our hearts by the Holy Spirit," we deliberately begin to identify ourselves with Jesus Christ's interests and purposes in others' lives (Romans 5:5). And Jesus has an interest in every individual person. We have no right in Christian service to be guided by our own interests and desires. In fact, this is one of the greatest tests of our relationship with Jesus Christ. The delight of sacrifice is that I lay down my life for my Friend, Jesus (see John 15:13). I don't throw my life away, but I willingly and deliberately lay it down for Him and His interests in other people. And I do this for no cause or purpose of my own. Paul spent his life for only one purpose—that he might win people to Jesus Christ. Paul always attracted people to his Lord, but never to himself. He said, "I have become all things to all men, that I might by all means save some" (1 Corinthians 9:22).

"You know that foreign rulers like to order their people around. And their great leaders have full power over everyone they rule. But don't act like them. If you want to be great, you must be the servant of all others. And if you want to be first, you must be the slave of all the rest. The Son of Man did not come to be a slave master, but a slave who would give his life to rescue many people". (Mathew 20: 26,27,28).

When someone thinks that to develop a holy life he must always be alone with God, he is no longer of any use to others. This is like putting himself on a pedestal and isolating himself from the rest of society. Many of us are interested only in our own goals, and Jesus cannot help. But if we are totally surrendered to Him, we have no goals of our own to serve.

The Lord inspires the aspirant to serve Him (by believing in His Existence). None else can do it. Such a one is His devotee, who is pleasing to Him. God blesses him with His Love. God is the Great Giver, ever so very Wise. There is no other like Him. He is the All-powerful Lord and Master; nobody knows how to worship Him. His Mansion is imperceptible. For ordinary mortals, it is so difficult to accept His Will. Says Nanak : "I have collapsed at Your Door, Lord. I am foolish and ignorant — please save me". [1185 SGGS]

The wandering beggars, warriors, celibates and hermit, through the Perfect Guru, consider this: without selfless service, no one ever receives the rewards.[992 SGGS]

That selfless servant, who lives in the Guru's household, is to obey the Guru's Commands. He is not to call attention to himself in any way. He is to meditate constantly within his heart on the Name of the Lord. One who sells his mind to the True Guru — that humble servant's affairs are resolved. One who performs selfless service, without thought of reward, shall attain his Lord and Master. He Himself grants His Grace; Says Nanak : that selfless servant practices the Guru's Teachings & Preachings.[286 SGGS]

This body is softened with the Guru's Word; one shall find peace, in selfless-service. The entire world continues to be affected by the force of reincarnation. Perform selfless-service, and you shall be given a place of honor in the Court of the Lord. Declares Nanak: now, swing your arms in joy! [25 SGGS]

Sharing is one of the basic tenets of Sikh Faith. Cooking and serving the holy food to the Congregation, then washing utensils, and dusting the shoes of the devotees is one kind of service; and there is the service of patients, disabled and aged.

John 21:17:The highest form of love is 'agape' (in Greek) love.
Let love be your only debt. If you love others, you have done all that
the Law (divine) demands: Be faithful in marriage, do not murder, and
do not steal. All of it is summed up in the command that says: love
others as much as you love yourself, no one who loves others shall
harm them (Romans 13: 8,9,10)

BROTHERLY LOVE The word that is usually rendered "brotherly
love" in the New Testament is the Greek *Philadelphia* and is used only
five times (Rom. 12:10; 1 Thess. 4:9; Heb. 13:1; 1 Pet. 1:22; 2 Pet.
1:7).

BELOVED DISCIPLE Term used only in John's Gospel to refer to a
disciple for whom Jesus had deep feelings. He has been variously
identified as Lazarus, an anonymous source or author of the Gospel, an
idealized disciple, or John's reference to himself without using his
own name.

BOND Used literally to speak of the bonds of prisoners or slaves
(Judg. 15:14; 1 Kings 14:10; Ps. 107:14; 116:16; Luke 8:29; Philem.
13). Used figuratively to speak of the bonds of wickedness or sin (Isa.
58:6; Luke 13:16; Acts 8:23), of affliction and judgment (Isa. 28:22;
52:2; Jer. 30:8; Nah. 1:13), the authority of kings (Job 12:18; Ps. 2:3),
the obligation to keep the covenant (Jer. 2:20; 5:5; see Col. 2:14), the
bonds of peace and love (Eph. 4:3; Col. 3:14), and the bonds of an evil
woman (Eccl. 7:26).

BRIDE Biblical writers have little to say about weddings or brides.
They occasionally mention means by which brides were obtained
(Gen. 24:4; 29:15-19). Ezekiel 16:8-14 describes bride, her attire, and
the wedding ceremony. The Song of Solomon is a collection of love
poems in which the bride describes her love for her bridegroom. The
imagery of the bride is used widely in the Bible as a description of the
people of God. In the Old Testament, the prophets presented Israel as a
bride who had committed repeated adulteries (Jer. 3; Ezek, 16; Hos.
3). (Jer. 33:10-11; Isa. 61:10, 62:5).

If the noose of emotional attachment binds humanity, then a devotee's love shall bind the Lord, with the bonds of his devotion and love. God cannot escape from a devotee's love-bondage; As for the mortal, he shall escape by worshipping and adoring God. The Lord is well aware of this. [658 SGGS]

The Power of Love has the potential of significantly changing one's overall perspective, for the betterment of self, and others. This new outlook could achieve wonders in all spheres of human-endeavour. All religious and spiritual deeds, sans Love, shall be rendered purposeless, in fact they shall be said to be exercises-in-futility. Love develops gradually, over a period of time, in everybody's life, as per varying circumstances, experiences and conducive-environment. Various instances of Love can be cited, in the Natural-realms. The blossoming of flowers, and the buzzing around of the bumblebee, are two examples. The peacock-dance is famous, at the sighting of rain-clouds. The love-pangs emanating from the heart of the timid partridge, pining for the Full Moon, are all manifestations of the hidden love, that is sublime and pristine, elevated and selfless, true and sacred. Love is such a magnetic- force, which attracts and influences everyone. Love is a state-of-the-mind. Its born inside the human heart, grows and develops, and on attaining maturity, assumes the form of affection, and the whole personality undergoes a metamorphic sea-change. The body and the mind, the heart and the soul, all, start reverberating with spiritually gifted strains-of-mellifluous-music. An unparalleled and inexplicable feeling of exhilaration engulfs the person. Anyone, who has never had this experience, this BOON, is really an unfortunate and condemned mortal. But, one must remain wary of all such people, who have a negative influence on one's life, even if those people are the closest relations or friends. Loving humanity is loving God.

FRIENDSHIP: A close trusting relationship between two people. Nowhere does the Bible present a concise definition of "friend" or "friendship." Instead, both the Old and New Testaments present friendship in its different facets. Two Hebrew root words, *r'h* and *ahv*, are used to describe friendship. *R'h* denotes an associate or companion, while *ahv* connotes the object of one's affection or devotion—a friend. Consequently, friendship may be simple association (Gen. 38:12; 2 Sam. 15:37) or loving companionship, the most recognizable example being that between David and Saul's son, Jonathan (1 Sam. 18:1, 3; 20:17; 2 Sam. 1:26). Friendship, however, was not limited to earthly associates.

The Old Testament also affirms friendship between God and human persons. And, even the New Testament affirms this, where Jesus says in the Book of John that all those who follow his commands are his friends.

FELLOWSHIP
The bond of common purpose and devotion that binds Christians together and to Christ. "Fellowship" is the English translation of words from the Hebrew stem *hbr* and the Greek stem *koin-*. The Hebrew *hbr* was used to express ideas such as common or shared house (Prov. 21:9), "binding" or "joining" (Ex. 26:6; Eccl. 9:4), companion (Eccl. 4:10), and even a wife as a companion (Mal. 2:14). *Haber* was used for a member of a Pharisaic society. Pharisees tended to form very close associations with one another in social, religious, and even business affairs.

79

None is my enemy, I'm everyone's friend. [1299 SGGS]

Nobody is to be considered an enemy, and one should not harbor animosity towards anyone. God, who expanded His expanse, is within all; this is the teaching imparted by the True Guru. Be a friend to all; when the sense of separation is removed from the mind, then unity with the Lord becomes easy, for the stubbornness is gone, Ambrosial Nectar rains down, and the Word of the Guru's Holy hymns seems sweet. He is pervading everywhere, in the water, on the land and in the sky; Nanak beholds the all-pervading Lord.[671 SGGS]

Such a persona is a friend, a companion, and the very best friend, who imparts the Teachings of the Lord. Nanak adores such a one, who chants the Name of the Lord.[298 SGGS]

If one makes friends with the self-willed ones, O friend, how can you expect peace? Make friends with the evolved souls, and focus the consciousness on the True Guru. The root of birth and death will be cut away, and then, one shall find peace, O friend. The Lord Himself instructs those who are misguided, when He casts His Glance of Grace. Those who are not blessed by His Glance of Grace, cry and weep and wail.[1421 SGGS]

Friendship is a 'jewel' that has unfathomable value.

The test of True friendship comes when one is in 'dire straits', and needs immediate help, whether in the form of advice, emotional-support, consolation, physical assistance, psychological-strength, financial support etc.

"If I am being poured out as a drink offering on the sacrifice and service of your faith, I am glad and rejoice with you all" (Philippians 2:17).

Are you willing to sacrifice yourself for the work of another believer—to pour out your life sacrificially for the ministry and faith of others? Or do you say, "I am not willing to be poured out right now, and I don't want God to tell me how to serve Him. I want to choose the place of my own sacrifice. And I want to have certain people watching me and saying, 'Well done.' "

Phil. 2:3 : "Do nothing from selfishness or empty conceit .... Let each of you regard one another more important than himself".
Phil. 2:4 : "Do not merely look out for your personal interests, but also for the interests of others".

It is one thing to follow God's way of service if you are regarded as a hero, but quite another thing if the road marked out for you by God requires becoming a "doormat" under other people's feet. God's purpose may be to teach you to say, "I know how to be abased ..." (Philippians 4:12). Are you ready to be sacrificed like that?

Are you ready to be less than a mere drop in the bucket—to be so totally insignificant that no one remembers you even if they think of those you served? Are you willing to give and be poured out until you are used up and exhausted—not seeking to be ministered to, but to minister? Some saints cannot do menial work while maintaining a saintly attitude, because they feel such service is beneath their dignity.

Do not delay in practicing righteousness; delay in committing sins. Implant the Name of the Lord, within oneself, and abandon greed. In the Sanctuary of the Saints, the sinful residues of past mistakes are erased. Meditating on the Lord, one shall become steady and stable. Nanak meditates on the Lord, for nothing and none else is permanent/stable, everything being variable, fluctuating, oscillating and temporary.[1354 SGGS]

There is none who could lay claim to achieving perfection, for GOD is the ONLY Perfect One. Blessed is the company of an emancipated soul. His mere glance has the potential of awarding peace and solace to a tormented being. Touching his Feet, one's conduct and lifestyle become pure. Abiding in his company, one chants the Lord's Praise, and reaches the Court of the Supreme Lord. Adhering to his teachings, one's thinking becomes revolutionized. The heart is contented, and the soul's aspirations are fulfilled. Such a Guru is perfect; his Teachings are everlasting. Beholding his Ambrosial Glance, one becomes saintly. Endless are his virtuous qualities, and his worth cannot be appraised. One who pleases him is united with Him. The tongue is one, but His Praises are countless. The True Lord of perfection cannot be assessed, is Incomprehensible, balanced in the state of Nirvaana. He is not sustained by food; He has no hatred or vengeance; He is the Giver of peace. Countless devotees continually bow in reverence to Him. In their hearts, they meditate on His Lotus Feet. One must always strive to enshrine His Pure Thoughts in one's mind, to attain a blessed life. Only GOD, does not contract or expand, HE does not become small or big, and, hence, is COMPLETE, TOTAL, and the ONLY PERFECT ONE. Anything incomplete becomes an eyesore, whether it's a statue, machinery, or furniture, because in that state it is of no consequence, and of no avail, for it cannot be put to any usage. An incomplete work of music, dance, prose or poetry is futile, as it cannot be enjoyed by anybody.

Binding and loosing, in this place, and in Matthew 16:19, is generally restrained, by Christian interpreters, to matters of discipline and authority. But it is as plain as the sun, by what occurs in numberless places dispersed throughout the Mishna, and from thence commonly used by the later rabbis when they treat of ritual subjects, that binding signified, and was commonly understood by the Jews at that time to be, a declaration that any thing was unlawful to be done; and loosing signified, on the contrary, a declaration that any thing may be lawfully done.

Sometimes God puts us through the experience and discipline of darkness to teach us to hear and obey Him. Songbirds are taught to sing in the dark, and God puts us into "the shadow of His hand" until we learn to hear Him (Isaiah 49:2). "Whatever I tell you in the dark …"—pay attention when God puts you into darkness, and keep your mouth closed while you are there. Are you in the dark right now in your circumstances, or in your life with God? If so, then remain quiet. If you open your mouth in the dark, you will speak while in the wrong mood—darkness is the time to listen. Don't talk to other people about it; don't read books to find out the reason for the darkness; just listen and obey. If you talk to other people, you cannot hear what God is saying. When you are in the dark, listen, and God will give you a very precious message for someone else once you are back in the light.

After every time of darkness, we should experience a mixture of delight and humiliation. If there is only delight, I question whether we have really heard God at all. We should experience delight for having heard God speak, but mostly humiliation for having taken so long to hear Him!

These eyes have seen a great many leave. All are worried about themselves, and so is Sheikh Fareed, the mystic, at his own plight. Lamenting, he says : if one reforms oneself, one shall meet God, and meeting Him, one shall be at peace. When a devotee becomes His, the whole world belongs to the devotee.[1382 SGGS]

Just as man likes to have decorated, organized and beautiful objects and people, so does God want to adopt only such humans, who are disciplined, in all senses of the word.   Only spiritually inclined, truthful, just, compassionate, morally and ethically clear people get the privilege of attaining Communion-with-GOD.

The entire Universe is functioning in consonance with the Laws & Discipline, enshrined in the Unwritten Constitution of the Nature, authored by GOD.

Bricks must be laid out, in a certain mode or array, in order that a straight wall be raised.   And, all mechanisms must function in accordance with a planned structure or design, involving operations and optimum utilization and desired results.

Similarly, the human body is a very complicated example of a machine, so intricately designed and organized.   Some functions are automatic, and remote-controlled (saliva-formation, perspiration, blood-circulation, urine and foecus-discharge, hormones, semen and sperm, the process of ovulation and child-birth etc.: the list is endless).

Other movements of the body are controlled by the nervous-system (brain) whose coordinate commands are received and implemented by the various sensory and motor organs.

Words, when organized in a certain fashion, yield the effect of poetry or prose. The disciplining of instruments and vocal-chords result in music.

Luke 17; 3, 4, 5 Correct any followers of mine who sin, and forgive the ones who say they are sorry. Even if one of them mistreats you, seven times in one day, and says "I am sorry", you should still forgive that person.

FORGIVENESS An act of God's grace to forget forever and not hold people of faith accountable for sins they confess; to a lesser degree the gracious human act of not holding wrong acts against a person. Forgiveness has both divine and human dimensions. In the divine relationship, it is, first of all, the gracious act of God by which believers are put into a right relationship to God and transferred from spiritual death to spiritual life through the sacrifice of Jesus. It is also, in this divine dimension, the ongoing gift of God without which our lives as Christians would be "out of joint" and full of guilt. In terms of a human dimension, forgiveness is that act and attitude toward those who have wronged us which restores relationships and fellowship.

Everyone Needs Forgiveness the basic facts of the Bible are God's creative power and holiness, human rebellion, and the efforts of our merciful God to bring us back to an intended relationship of sonship and fellowship. The need of forgiveness is first seen in the third chapter of Genesis, as Adam and Eve willfully disobeyed God, choosing rather to satisfy their own self-will. The result was guilt (Gen. 3:8, 10), separation from God, loss of fellowship (Gen. 3:8, 23-24), and a life of hardship, anxiety, and death (Gen. 3:16-24) lived under the wrath of God. Old Testament: The principal word used to express kindness in the Old Testament bears the connotation of a loyal love, which manifests itself not in emotions but in actions. Rahab expected kindness in return for her kindness to the spies (Josh. 2:12, 14). Joseph expected kindness from the cupbearer in return for the interpretation of a dream (Gen. 40:14).

My Lord forgives innumerable sins, in seconds. [260 SGGS]
To practice forgiveness is the true form of fasting, good conduct and
contentment. Disease does not afflict one, nor does the pain of death.
One is liberated, and absorbed into God, who has no form or feature.
[223 SGGS]
Searching, endlessly, when one finally drinks the Ambrosial Nectar.
Then, adopting the way of tolerance, one surrenders one's mind to the
True Guru.[932 SGGS]

Abide in truth and contentment, O humble Siblings of Destiny. Hold
tight to compassion and the Sanctuary of the True Guru. Knowing
one's soul, and knowing the Supreme Soul; associating with the Guru,
one shall be emancipated.[1030 SGGS]

If the soul-bride adorns herself with compassion and forgiveness, God
is pleased, and her mind is illumined with the lamp of the Guru's
wisdom. With happiness and ecstasy, God enjoys her; She offers her
soul to Him.[836 SGGS]

Those who have truth as their fast, contentment as their sacred shrine
of pilgrimage, spiritual wisdom and meditation as their cleansing
bath, kindness as their deity, and forgiveness as their chanting beads,
are the really emancipated souls. Those who adopt the Way of the
Lord, as their loin-cloth, and intuitive awareness as their
ritualistically purified enclosure, and good deeds as their ceremonial
fore-head mark, such souls, says Nanak, are very rare. [1245 SGGS]

Without patience and forgiveness, countless hundreds of thousands
have perished. Their numbers cannot be counted; none could count
them. By the blessing of the Lord's Word, enter the Mansion of the
Lord's Presence; one shall be blessed with patience, forgiveness, truth
and peace. And one shall be unfettered. Partake of the true wealth of
meditation, and the Lord Himself shall abide within one's body.
Through egotism, one is distracted and ruined; other than the Lord, all
things are corrupt. Forming His creatures, He placed Himself within
them; the Creator is unattached and infinite.[937 SGGS]

COMPASSION To feel passion with someone, to enter sympathetically into his or her sorrow and pain. Compassion in English translations represents at least five Hebrew and eight Greek terms. *Chamal* means "to regret," "be sorry for," "grieve over," or "spare someone." Thus the rich man "refrained" (NIV) from taking his own sheep and took the poor man's (2 Sam. 12:4). Pharaoh's daughter "had pity" on the baby Moses (Ex. 2:6). David spared Mephibosheth for Jonathan's sake (2 Sam. 21:7). Often it expresses God's anger and decision no longer to show mercy and pity (Zech. 11:6). Beyond this the Bible points to God's plans to again have compassion for His people (Joel 2:18; compare Mal. 3:17; Gen. 19:16; 2 Chron. 36:15; Isa. 63:9).

Chen represents what is aesthetically beautiful. It means then to possess grace and charm and to be gracious. God looked to pour out a spirit of grace or "compassion" (Zech. 12:10 NRSV) on His people so they would mourn for the one they pierced. Bildad told Job to "implore the compassion of the Almighty" (Job 8:5 NASB).

2:18-23 on sharing this grain with her mother-in-law, Ruth reports that it was Boaz who gave her such favored treatment as she worked. Encouraged to continue this relationship, Ruth remains in Boaz' fields until the end of both the barley and the wheat harvests, a period of about seven weeks (Deut 16:9-12).

8:1-7 God's grace in bestowing salvation through Christ and the gifts of the Spirit on the Macedonian community (see note on Rom 15:26) led to their generous contribution in spite of their ordeal of affliction (Phil 1:29-30; 1 Thess 1:6; 2:14; 3:3-4; Acts 17:1-11). Sharing in Greek means mutual participation and is called a ministry to the saints in Jerusalem (1 Cor 16:15; 2 Cor 9:1, 12, 13; Rom 15:25, 31).

Make compassion the cotton, contentment the thread, modesty the knot and truth the twist. If this is the sacred thread that the priest has to offer, for the soul, then one must wear it. It does not break, it cannot be soiled by filth, and it cannot be burnt, or lost. Blessed are those mortal beings, says Nanak, who wear such a thread around their necks. One buys the ordinary thread for a few shells, and seated in an enclosure, one wears it. Whispering instructions into others' ears, the priest becomes a guru. But the recipient dies, and the sacred thread falls away, and the soul departs without it. [471 SGGS]

One who works for what he eats, and gives some of what he has, says Nanak, he knows the Path.[1245 SGGS]

Compassion and contentment are intertwined-entities. Both lend discipline to Life. Only a compassionate person would be of service to others, and only a contented person could meditate, in tranquility and serenity. An uncontented person shall always be complaining of the lack of everything, in life (wealth, children, comforts, status), or about everything that went wrong (losses, ill-health, etc.). God likes contented people, and answers their prayers. HE grants them certain special powers of healing others, and bestows, upon them, certain skills and talents, which even some learned and experienced persons might lack, and envy. It's then that the ornamentation of the 'Bride' becomes complete, replete with God's Name.

Religion, sans compassion and meditation and service, is like a 'corpse', rotten in substance, and releasing odours, despised by all. The sight of a compassionate person is equivalent to bathing at the places of pilgrimage, in the holy waters. Without compassion, all service is a hoax. This, then, cannot be termed as an exemplary service to humankind. There would be eternal bliss in any selfless service performed with compassion. Without contentment, meditation becomes another ordinary ritual done according to a routine schedule, and ritual gives birth to egocentrism of the worst kind.

HUMILITY :   The Old Testament connects the quality of humility with Israel's lowly experience as slaves in Egypt—a poor, afflicted, and suffering people (Deut. 26:6). The Hebrew word translated, as humility is similar to another Hebrew word meaning "to be afflicted." In Old Testament thought, humility was closely associated with individuals who were poor and afflicted (2 Sam. 22:28). What God desires most is not outward sacrifices but a humble spirit (Psa. 51:17; Mic. 6:8). Such a humble spirit shows itself in several ways: (1) a recognition of one's sinfulness before a holy God (Isa. 6:5); (2) obedience to God (Deut. 8:2); and (3) submission to God (2 Kings 22:19; 2 Chron. 34:37).

The Old Testament promised blessings to those who were humble: (1) wisdom (Prov. 11:2); (2) good tidings (Isa. 61:1); and (3) honor (Prov. 15:33).   The experience of many kings indicated that those who humble themselves before God would be exalted (1 Kings 21:29; 2 Kings 22:19; 2 Chron. 32:26; 33:12, 19). Those who do not humble themselves before God will be afflicted (2 Chron. 33:23; 36:12). New Testament Jesus Christ's life provides the best example of what it means to have humility (Matt. 11:29; 1 Cor. 4:21; Phil. 2:1-11). Jesus preached and taught often about the need for humility (Matt. 23:12; Mark 9:35; Luke 14:11; 18:14). He urged those who desired to live by Kingdom standards to practice humility (Matt. 18:1; 23:12). The person with humility does not look down on others (Matt. 18:4; Luke 14:11). Humility in the New Testament is closely connected with the quality of "meekness" (Matt. 5:5). While God resists those who are proud, He provides grace for the humble (Jas. 4:6). Primary in the New Testament is the conviction that one who has humility will not be overly concerned about his or her prestige (Matt. 18:4; 23:12; Rom. 12:16; 2 Cor. 11:7).

One must become as humble as grass, if one longs to enter the Court of the Lord, as grass is cut, trampled over and remains under others' feet; [1378 SGGS]

The simmal tree is straight as an arrow; it is very tall, and very thick. But those birds, which visit it hopefully, depart disappointed. Its fruits are tasteless, its flowers are nauseating, and its leaves are useless. Sweetness and humility, Says Nanak, are the essence of virtue and goodness. When something is placed on the balancing scale and weighed, the side that descends is heavier. The sinner, like the deer hunter, bows down twice as much. But what can be achieved by bowing the head, when the heart is impure? [470 SGGS]

Among all, the supreme person is the one who gives up egotistical pride in the Company of the Holy; one who considers oneself as lowly, shall be accounted as the highest of all. One whose mind is the dust of all, recognizes the Name of the Lord,, in each and every heart. One who eradicates cruelty from within his own mind, looks upon the entire world as his friend, affirms Nanak, is not affected by sin or virtue. [266 SGGS]

All that we eat is worthless if it is not accrued from a life of dignity and honor [201 SGGS].

Therefore, is only justified, and quite justiciable, that one fights for one's due rights, after exercising restraint to a certain extent. Humility must not be misconstrued to imply weakness of any sort.

If one becomes the slave of the Lord's slaves, then he finds the Lord, and eradicates ego from within. The Lord of bliss is his object of devotion; night and day, he sings the Glorious Praises of the Lord. Humility must not be misconstrued to imply timidity and weakness. It is, on the contrary, a powerful characteristic, that speaks volumes about the humble one's personality. The humble person is bestowed fame and fortune, even without asking (praying) for it. On the other hand, someone who seeks recognition, on account of one's wealth, status or knowledge, is not a humble person. Occasionally, one needs to remind oneself, of the destructibility of the human-body (by looking downwards, towards the earth, and at the dust and ashes, unto which this body shall merge).

Romans 15: 1 if our faith is so strong, we should be patient with the Lord's followers whose faith is weak. We should try to please them instead of ourselves. We should try to help them.

CONSOLATION Comfort, which eases grief and pain. The Hebrew terms are closely related to the words for compassion—*nichum, nocham.* See Compassion. Job's integrity with God's instructions gave him consolation despite his grief and pain (Job 6:10). David sent servants to console Hanun, king of Ammon, after his father died (2 Sam. 10:1-2). People brought food and drink to console the grieving (Jer. 16:7; compare John 11:19). God's response to prayer brings consolation to the worried soul (Ps. 94:19). Even as God destroyed Jerusalem, He provided consolation in the person of faithful survivors (Ezek. 14:22-23).

Mathew 21: 20 : The disciples were shocked when they saw how quickly the tree had dried up. But Jesus said to them : "If you have faith and don't doubt, I promise that you can do what I did to this tree. And you will be able to do even more. You can tell this mountain to get up and jump into the sea, and it will. If you have faith when you pray, you will be given whatever you ask for".

Israel's ultimate hope was the consolation only the Messiah could bring. The faithful waited expectantly for this (Luke 2:25; compare Isa. 40:1-2). Those who trust in riches rather than in the coming of the Son of Man have all the consolation they will receive (Luke 6:24). Believers receive consolation through the ministry of proclamation (1 Cor. 14:3). Lord, as this leper may be considered as a fit emblem of the corruption of man by sin; so may his cure, of the redemption of the soul by Christ. A penitent sinner seeks God with a respectful faith; approaches him in the spirit of adoration; humbles himself under his mighty hand, acknowledging the greatness of his fall.

One who has faith in the Guru comes to dwell upon God. He is acclaimed as a devotee, a humble devotee throughout the three worlds. The Lord resides in his heart. True are his actions; true are his ways. True is his heart; Truth is what he utters. True is his vision; true is his form. He distributes Truth and he spreads Truth. One who recognizes the Supreme Lord as The True ONE, that humble being immerses himself, in meditation, and merges his identity with THE SOLE ENTITY. [283 SGGS]

And, this trust prods one onto realization of the self, and one's roots, which ultimately results in God-realization.

One must try, always, to remain in a state of equilibrium and stability, and never to let dilemma invade the mind. That's possible only when one tends to have an abiding faith in the Guru's sayings (Word / Command / Advice). On that foundation is the marvellous palace, having bejeweled walls, raised. Such a devotee is entitled to be the recipient of lavish eulogies and encomiums, all over, on the surface of earth, and has a rare and unique glow and radiance, on his face.[678 SGGS]

Like, faith in Water leads one to the ultimate hope of thirst being quenched on drinking it. And, like faith in Sun reassures the needy, that its warmth shall prove to be comforting, on a cold, chilly-night, in the winters, Faith in the Supreme-Reality would lead one to the fulfillment of all worldly desires. And, finally, this faith and trust would assist the bearer, to be ferried across the Ocean-of-Fire (Life), in a befitting and honorable fashion. This would be Salvation, for an aspiring Soul.

Miraculous powers have known to be associated with the saga of Samson, according to the following quotations from the Bible.

Judges 13-3-5 : And Samson was born : Manoah, from the tribe of 'Dan' lived in the town of Zorah. His wife was unable to bear children.

Then, an Angel heralded the conception, and told her; "You have never been able to have a son, but, very soon you shall bear one", and advised her to NEVER cut his hair, for he would belong to GOD, the time he is begotten of her, hence the child must live in HIS image. And, the child thus born came to be known as Samson.

Later, during his lifetime, Samson testified to this Truth. On being enquired by Delilah, Samson's beloved, he confides unto her thus : "I have belonged to God ever since I was born, and my hair has never been cut off; if it were ever cut off, my strength would leave me, and I would be as weak as anyone else".

When Samson was imprisoned, his hair was cut, and his strength diminished. Later, in due course, when the hair grew again, his powers returned, enabling him to face and kill several thousands of his foes.

Numbers 6-5: RULES FOR NAZARITES : Even the hair of a Nazarite is sacred, and he must NEVER cut it. The Lord commanded Moses to proclaim to the Israelites that they must retain hair in order to prove their loyalty and devotion to the Lord, for hair is considered to be sacred, and a symbol of being holy.

Furthermore, Lord Jesus is always shown having hair, in all portraits, paintings, sculptures etc.

According to Sri Guru Granth Sahib, hair retention which has always been held as a prerequisite to called a Sikh, as it is a gift from God, is known to possess miraculous powers, symbol of saintliness, devotion and extreme humility.

"He gives Support to the unsupported. The Name of the Lord is the Wealth of the poor. The Lord of the Universe is the Master of the masterless; the Beautiful-haired Lord is the Power of the weak". (Pg.1355 SGGS).

*"Beautiful are God's eyes, beautiful are His teeth, graceful are His nose and long **hair**".* (Pg.567 SGGS)

*"My mind is the dust of the feet of the Holy. The Guru has implanted the Sweet Name of the Lord, within me. I dust the Guru's Feet with my **hair**".* (Pg.1335 SGGS).

*"I make my **hair** into a fan, and wave it over the Saint. I bow my head low, to touch his feet, and apply his dust to my face".* (Pg.745) SGGS

*"I perform service for Your slave, O Lord, and wipe his feet with my **hair**. I offer my head to him, and listen to the Glorious Praises of the Lord, the source of bliss".* (Pg.810 SGGS).

*"I chant the Name of the Beautifully-**haired** Lord; do not sleep unaware. Chanting His Name night and day, the Lord will eventually hear your call".* (Pg.1376 SGGS).

All Sikh Gurus and their disciples have always retained unshorn hair.

ETHICS The study of good behavior, motivation, and attitude in light of Jesus Christ and biblical revelation. The discipline of ethics deals with such questions as: "What ought I do?" "How should I act so as to do what is good and right?" "What is meant by good?" "Who is the good person?"

Biblical ethics likewise addresses some of the identical questions. While neither Testament has an abstract, comprehensive term or definition which parallels the modern term "ethics," both the Old Testament and the New Testament are concerned about the manner of life that the Scripture prescribes and approves. The closest Hebrew term in the Old Testament for "ethics," "virtue" or "ideals" is the word *musar*, "discipline" or "teaching" (Prov. 1:8) or even *derek*, "way or path" of the good and the right. The closest parallel Greek term in the New Testament is *anastrophe*, "way of life, life-style" (occurring nine times in a good sense with 2 Pet. 3:11 being the most significant usage). Of course the Greek terms *ethos* or *ethos* appear twelve times in the New Testament (Luke 1:9; 2:42; 22:39; John 19:40; Acts 6:14; 15:1; 16:21; 21:21; 25:16; 26:3; 28:17 and Heb. 10:25). The plural form appears once in 1 Corinthians 15:33. It is usually translated "conduct," "custom," "manner of life," or "practice."

God's Kingdom is steady, stable and eternal. There is no second or third status; all are equal there. That city is populous and eternally famous. Those who live there are wealthy and contented. They stroll about freely, just as they please, and no one blocks their way. [345 SGGS]

The Twin-Concepts are based on the express premise that an ideal society can thrive and survive only when the individuals, who constitute it, are contented, prosperous and happy. Only then could higher attainments be probable, in other fields like religion and spirituality. Without the basic requirements being fulfilled, one can never have the peace-of-mind, a pre-requisite for Sincere Devotion & Meditation, which frame-of-mind would, then, prod one onto the path of expanding one's horizons, to think of the humanity, at large. The Ruler, King or the Establishment/Government should be endowed with such qualities, that the subjects could repose their trust and confidence, in that authority, without any fear or doubt, whatsoever. The Keyword, here, must be "SERVICE", and NOT "TYRANNY". Only if the reign is democratic and secular and tolerant and just shall it survive long enough.

The 4 basic Postulates for a Contented Life thus formulated are: ***Piety, Wealth, Desire-Fulfillment, & Final-Emancipation.***

All of these can be accomplished, and enjoyed, even while leading the regular life of a householder. The position and relevance of womenfolk, in the 'body-politik' and social-structure is of paramount import and significance. A woman deserves the honor and esteem that has been denied to her, for a long time, only until recently, when the winds of change brought about a "Renaissance & Revolution", for the betterment of humanity. The reverential treatment, given to women, now, is the ideal that the THIRD NANAK, Guru Amar Das had propounded forcefully, centuries ago. An individual must be strong, in all respects: spiritual, moral, religious, social, mental, psychological, emotional, financial.

Mark 10: 21 Jesus looked closely at the man. He liked him, and said: "There is one thing you still need to do. Go sell everything you own. Give the money to the poor, and you will have riches in heaven. Then come with me".

MERCHANT Buyer and seller of goods for profit. With the exception of the period of Solomon (1 Kings 9:26-28; 10:15, 22), Israel was not known in biblical times as a nation of merchants. References to Israelites involved in trade are surprisingly few. Israelites were prohibited from selling food to fellow Israelites for profit (Lev. 25:37), but could sell even carrion to a foreigner (Deut. 14:21). Merchants purchased cloth from housewives (Prov. 31:24). olive oil was sold (2 Kings 4:7). Abuses by merchants were often condemned: holding back grain to force up prices (Prov. 11:26); impatience for sabbath or holy days to conclude so that commerce might resume; dishonest scales (Amos 8:5); forcing fellow Israelites into slavery to buy food (Neh. 5:1-8); violation of the Sabbath (Neh. 13:15-21). Jerusalem merchants assisted in Nehemiah's reconstruction of the walls, perhaps by providing finances (Neh. 3:32). The majority of Old Testament references to merchants concern nations other than Israel.

The term translated as merchant or trader at Proverbs 31:24 and Hosea 12:7 is, in fact, the word for Canaanite. They traded in common and precious metals, slaves, livestock, precious stones, ivory, wool, cloth, clothing, agricultural produce, wine, spices, and carpets. (Compare Rev. 18:11-13.) Tyre's trading partners included twenty-two nations or peoples encompassing Asia Minor, Palestine, Syria, Arabia, and Mesopotamia. Merchants generated great wealth. The prophets railed against the pride which accompanied merchants' material successes (Isa. 23; Ezek. 27). In the New Testament, Jesus used a merchant to illustrate the need to risk all to gain the kingdom of heaven (Matt. 13:45-46.

Make all deals, O' traders, and take good care of the merchandise. Buy that object which will go along, to the next world. In the next world, the All-knowing Merchant will take this object and shall reward the earthly trader. Take the Merchandise of the Lord's Praises along. The Lord shall see this and approve. Those who do not have the Assets of Truth—how can they find peace? Like the deer caught in the trap, they suffer in terrible agony; they continually cry out in pain. The counterfeit coins are not put into the Treasury; they do not obtain the Blessed Vision of the Lord-Guru. Practicing falsehood again and again, people come and go in reincarnation, and forfeit their honor. Advises Nanak: Those who chant the Name of the Lord earn great profits.[22 SGGS]

Praise the Formless Lord in the mind. O my mind, make this the true occupation. Let the tongue become pure, to taste the Ambrosial Nectar. And then the soul shall be, forever, peaceful. The Company of the Holy is the all-important one. Hence, perform the tasks assigned by the Lord, and listen to the Lord's Sermon. In the Lord's Court, such a face shall be radiant, so Promises Nanak.[81 SGGS]

With greed within them, their minds are filthy, and they spread filth around. They indulge in filthy deeds, and suffer in pain. They deal in falsehood, and nothing but falsehood; telling lies, they suffer in pain. Rare is that person who enshrines the Immaculate Guru's Word within his mind. By Guru's Grace, his skepticism is removed. He walks in harmony with the Guru's Will, day and night; remembering the Name of the Lord, he attains peace. [1062 SGGS]

An ideal business is one from whose profits, society benefits. Such a businessperson is God's chosen one. His service to humanity, and his humanism shall be the cause of receiving rewards, forever, financially, and spiritually.

It is the custom, even in circles where the full supernatural claims of Christianity are not admitted, to speak of Christ's religion as, in comparison with others, "the *absolute* religion, absolute truth" meaning by this that in Christianity the true idea of religion, which in other faiths is only striven after, attains to complete and final expression. Hegel, e.g. speaks of Christianity as the "Absolute or Revealed Religion" in the sense that in it the idea is discovered of the essential unity of God and man (Thus also T. H. Green, E. Caird, etc.); others (e.g. Pfleiderer) in the meaning that it expresses the absolute "principle" of religion—a Divine sonship. Christianity also claims for itself, though in a more positive way, to be the absolute religion. It is the final and perfect revelation of God for which not only revelation in Israel, but the whole providential history of the race, was a Divinely ordained preparation (Gal 4:4).

RELATION OF CHRISTIANITY TO ETHNIC FAITHS AND THEIR TENETS

It is very remarkable that Christianity—though clearly not a philosophy but a religion that has arisen under historical circumstances which preclude the possibility of supposing it the product of Eclecticism—yet sums up in itself all that is good in all religions and philosophies, without the bad, the fearful perversions and corruptions of the moral sense, too often found in them. The more the study of comparative religion is carried on the more plainly evident does this become. It also supplements in a wonderful way the half-truths concealed rather than revealed in other systems, whether religious or philosophical.

From the One Light, the entire universe welled up. So who is good, and who is bad? : First, God created the Light; then, by His Creative Power, He made all mortal beings. The Creation is in the Creator, and the Creator is in the Creation, totally pervading and permeating all places. The clay is the same, but the Potter has fashioned it in various ways. The One True Lord abides in all; Says Kabeer, his anxiety and fear have been taken away; he sees the Immaculate Lord pervading everywhere. Do not say that the Vedas, the Bible and the Koran are false. Those who do not contemplate them are false.[1349 SGGS]

Just ponder: Whom should we call good or bad? Joining the Guru's Congregation, and one comes in God's proximity. The ones with Godly-attributes are immaculately pure; no filth sticks to them. Says Nanak : the Name of the Lord, abides in the heart, by the greatest pre-ordained destiny. [353 SGGS]

In the dwelling of the womb, there is no ancestry or social status. All have originated from the Seed of God. If one is indeed a Brahmin (considered to be one of the highest castes in Hindu society), born of a Brahmin mother, then why didn't one come by some other way? How is it that one is a Brahmin, and another of a low social status? How is it that one is formed of blood, and another made of milk? Says Kabeer : one who contemplates God, is said to be a Brahmin (the learned and the wise, on account of merit, and not due to caste or class) among us. [324 SGGS]

The Sikh Scripture, Sri Guru Granth Sahib emphasizes, categorically, that ALL religions and faiths propagate the exemplary virtues and guidelines, so very essential for leading a purposeful and fulfilled life. And the various Prophets and Seers, belonging to diverse schools-of-thought, were unanimous in their spiritual-beliefs. It is the devilish tendency of the human mind that 'conceives and delivers the deformed baby' of rift and conflict, of mistrust and discord.

But he said, Nay—God judges quite otherwise than men of this mixture of good and evil in the world; he knows the good which he intends to produce from it, and how far his patience towards the wicked should extend, in order to their conversion, or the farther sanctification of the righteous. Men often persecute a true Christian, while they intend only to prosecute an impious person. "A zeal for the extirpation of heretics and wicked men," said a pious Papist, "not regulated by these words of our blessed Savior, allows no time for the one to grow strong in goodness, or to the other to forsake their evil courses. They are of a spirit very opposite to his, who care not if they root up the wheat, provided they can but gather up the tares." The zeal that leads persons to persecute others for religious opinions is not less a seed of the devil than a bad opinion itself is.

Have patience with me: be long-minded towards me—give me longer space. The means, which a sinner should use to be saved, are: (1) Deep humiliation of heart—he fell down. (2) Fervent prayer. (3) Confidence in the mercy of God—have patience. (4) A firm purpose to devote his soul and body to his Maker, I   will pay thee all.   Of the good and faithful servants he approves, and therefore exalts them to his glory; of the slothful and wicked he disapproves, and casts them into hell.

SHEEP, which have ever been considered as the emblems of mildness, simplicity, patience, and usefulness, represent here the genuine Disciples of Christ.   Math.25: GOATS, which are naturally quarrelsome, lascivious, and excessively ill scented, were considered as the symbols of riotous, profane, and impure men. They here represent all who have lived and died in their sins. See Ezekiel 34:17, and Zechariah 10:3.   Sheep have also been classified as: 'wayward and/or stupid'.

She should make the Lord, the Slayer of demons, her ring, and take the Transcendent Lord as her silken clothes. The soul-bride should weave patience into the braids of her hair, and apply the lotion of the Lord, the Great Lover. If she lights the lamp in the mansion of her mind, and makes her body the nuptial-bed of the Lord, then, when the King of spiritual wisdom comes to her bed, He shall accept her, and she shall experience an ecstatic bliss.[359 SGGS]

Patience, glory and honor are bestowed upon those who listen to the Name of the Lord. That yearning soul, whose heart remains merged with the Lord, says Nanak, obtains glorious greatness. [257 SGGS]

"Work for your Lord and Master; dispel the doubts of your heart. The humble devotees, have the strength and endurance of trees".[1381 SGGS]

The God-conscious being has a steady patience, like the earth, which bears the ignominy and cruelty of being dug up by one, but is later anointed with sandal paste by another (the soil is worshipped in some cultures and religions).[272 SGGS]

Patience is a virtue that brings us closer to God.

In today's strife-torn environment, tolerance and patience is the key.

Section 3

Tug of War

Since time, immemorial,
there have been opposing
'currents, trends, and tendencies',
as it is in the nature of the Universe;
whether it is religious belief and political
perception, or the domination of man over
woman, or the difference of opinion in
adopting the noble attributes in life.

HUMANITY The characteristics which unite all persons despite their many individual differences and constitute them as God's "image."
Theologians have supposed that this "image" designates what is most essential to human nature. Many patristic, Catholic, and Protestant orthodox theologians have argued that the image was reason. Although Scripture depicts humans as thinking creatures, this definition was originally derived from Greek philosophy. More accurate is the suggestion that the image consists in humankind's lordship over and stewardship of creation, for this is the theme of the following verses (Gen. 1:28-31).

The best clue comes from frequent reference to Jesus as that image to which we are to be conformed (Rom. 8:29; 1 Cor. 15:49; 2 Cor. 3:18; 4:4). The most basic characteristics of Jesus' life were His dependence upon and devotion to His Father and His loving servant hood toward His fellow humans. This suggests that the essence of being human consists in a three-fold relationship: towards God as Lord, towards other humans as fellow servants, and towards creation as entrusted to our care. The second feature is confirmed by Genesis 1:27 which, as Karl Barth noticed, practically identifies being in God's image with being female and male. For in the interdependence between the sexes, the need, desire, and delight of humans for and in each other can be most vividly symbolized.

Theologians have often discussed whether individual humans are composed of just body and soul, or of body, soul, and spirit. Yet this question has been somewhat misguided. Scripture represents people not as individuals composed of parts, but as integrated, acting units intimately interrelated with others.

Woman and Man are complements, as well as supplements, to each other. The mutual attraction between the two magnetic fields is, but, natural, because man has certain female hormones/genes in him, and vice -versa.

The female is in the male, and the male is in the female. Understand this, O God-realized being! The focus of attention is on the celestial music of God's Noumenon, resulting in the realization of Almighty's power. [879 SGGS]

The insatiable appetite for power and authority has led man to assume the leadership-roles in a variety of spheres of endeavor, namely politics, religion, business, warfare, and the larger society, in general. Some thinkers and philosophers, naturally men, had the courage to classify women as "Insignificant, irrelevant ones". Women were castigated, oppressed, subjugated, tortured, exploited in all manners, possible, and were relegated to the background, in all matters.
Guru Nanak was the first religious preacher who raised his voice against the tyranny and indignation suffered by women, over the ages.

Woman bears a male child; within woman, man is conceived; to woman he is engaged and married. Woman becomes his friend; through woman, the future generations come. So why call her low? She gives birth to kings. From woman, woman is born; without woman, there would be no one at all. Only the True Lord is excluded from the womb's cycle of birth and death. [473 SGGS]

The woman's contribution to society cannot and must not be ignored. Her role has to be recognized by the males. The human-frame is a temple, constructed by God, Himself, and the home is a Temple of Understanding, created jointly, by woman and man. Only when mutual love and care are shared, with humility and grace, witnessing God in each other, shall their home and family be blessed, where peace, harmony, serenity, and tranquility shall prevail.

Peter's wife's mother-Learn hence, says Theophylact, that marriage is no hindrance to virtue, since the chief of the apostles had his wife. Marriage is one of the first of Divine Institutions, and is a positive command of God. He says, the state of celibacy is not GOOD (Genesis 2:18). Those who pretend to say that the single state is more holy than the other. Slander their Maker, and say, in effect, that they are too holy to listen the Commandments. Mathew 8:15 -He touched her hand-can anything on this side of the unlimited power of God effect such a cure with only a touch? If the Scriptures had not spoken about the divinity of Christ, these proofs of his power must have demonstrated it to the common sense of every man whose creed had not previously blinded him. Marriage is one of the first of Divine institutions, and is a positive command of God. He says, the state of celibacy is not GOOD, Genesis 2:18.

DIVORCE : From early time provision was made for divorce among the Israelites (Deut. 24:1-4). Presumably prior to this decree, a wife could be put out of the home at the pleasure of the husband. This gave some dignity and protection to the divorced woman. The passage in Deuteronomy did not give clear guidelines. "Because he hath found some uncleanness in her" (Deut. 24:1) left room for interpretation. One group of rabbis insisted that divorce could be granted only if the wife was immoral. Another group argued that divorce could be secured by the husband if the wife displeased him in any way.

On another occasion as Jesus taught about divorce (Matt. 5:31-32), He referred to the passage in Deuteronomy 24 as common knowledge among His hearers. He did not give His approval to the practice of divorce. Rather, He showed the consequences of divorce in the lives of people. If a man divorced his wife, he made her an adulteress unless the basis of the divorce was her own immorality. This statement has been understood in various ways. One idea is that Jesus was giving here a justifiable ground for divorce. If the wife violated her marriage vows, the husband had the right to divorce her. A divorced woman in Palestine of that day had few choices. To survive she could remarry or become a prostitute. In either case she was guilty of adultery.

As per Sikh customs/traditions, as governed by the religious-spiritual Diktat of the Gurus, woman and man undertake to tie the nuptial-knot, according to the prescribed code-of-conduct. They must reciprocate love and understanding, while taking due care of recognizing each other's and uniqueness, thereby ensuring equality (as equals, and as life-partners). This shall eliminate any occurrence of conflict on the basis of a perceived threat to either's identity. Harmony shall prevail, and all crisis situations shall be dealt with, in a spirit of compromise, and commitment shall keep divorce at bay. The ascending divorce-rate, in the Western Society & Culture, is attributable to the fact that the institution of marriage is considered to be no more than a Legal-Contract, that can be nullified, with the stroke of the pens of the two parties and a Judge. Both must strive to achieve a state of camaraderie, at all planes: emotional, physical, financial, intellectual, and spiritual. Celibacy has been repudiated in the strongest terms, for it is well nigh impossible to banish the thought of sexual-union.

To have religious sanction, the ceremony is to be solemnized in the presence of the Holy Congregation, where the bride and the groom are required to circumbulate the Scripture, four times, as the priest reads the appropriate hymn.

In the first round, the Lord sets forth Instructions for performing duties of married life. Embrace the Conduct of Righteousness, renouncing sin. Enshrine the contemplative remembrance of God, in your hearts. Second round, the Lord leads both to meet the True Guru, the Primal Being. The Fear of the Fearless Lord in the mind eradicates the filth of egotism. The bride prepares to start a new life, in a new home, on leaving her parental abode. Third round, the mind is filled with Divine Love. In the fourth and final round, the emphasis is on Unison, between the spouses, as also Communion between God and Human-Soul. She has attained her Lord and Master, the cherished fruit of her mind's desires. [773 SGGS]

God formed man of the dust—In the most distinct manner God shows us that man is a compound being, having a body and soul distinctly, and separately created; the body out of the dust of the earth, the soul immediately breathed from God himself. Does not this strongly mark that the soul and body are not the same thing? The body derives its origin from the earth, the dust; hence because it is earthly it is decomposable and perishable. Of the soul it is said, God breathed into his nostrils the breath of life; the breath of LIVES, i.e., animal and intellectual. While this breath of God expanded the lungs and set them in play, his inspiration gave both spirit and understanding.

Thou shalt surely die—a death thou shalt die; or, dying thou shalt die. Thou shalt not only die spiritually, by losing the life of God, but from that moment thou shalt become mortal, and shalt continue in a dying state till thou die. This we find literally accomplished; every moment of man's life may be considered as an act of dying, till soul and body are separated.

Death in the Synoptic Gospels and Acts Several passages in the Synoptic Gospels (Matthew, Mark, and Luke) and Acts imply a positive, or at least neutral, attitude toward death. In Luke's birth narrative, for example, Simeon asked God to let him "depart in peace" because he had seen God's salvation (2:29). Similar to the Old Testament accounts of some of the patriarchs, Simeon's death would be the peaceful resignation of a life dedicated to God. In a Sermon on the Mount saying (Matt. 6:27; Luke 12:25), Jesus counseled His listeners with a rhetorical question, "and which of you by being anxious can add a single cubit to his life's span" ?

Only this is the chance, a golden one at that. Just ponder, and analyze, hypothetically, this very moment, for later you might lose this opportunity, and then, nothing more than a sordid feeling of remorse and repentance shall remain, in the heart.[1159 SGGS]

All that is seen must die. Only God and his devotees are spiritually immortal. [1100 SGGS]

(This 'CHANCE' pertains to the optimum and best utilization of this lifetime, for meditation, and for doing good to others. One's own welfare would be a natural consequence, and a foregone conclusion).

First conquer the fear of death, learn to accept/embrace death; only then would you become worthy of living a pristinely sublime and selfless life. Humility and faith in God would result in fortitude.

First, accept death, and give up any hope of life. Becoming the dust of the feet of all, and then, one may come to GOD. Accept that only one who has died, truly lives, and one who is alive, consider him dead. Those who are in love with the One Lord, are the blessed ones. Pain does not even approach that person, within whose mind God resides. Hunger and thirst do not affect him, and the Messenger of Death does not terrorize him. [1102 SGGS]

Whomsoever discovered this treasure-chest of Noumenon, his treasury shall overflow with piety, humility, prosperity and service.

Practicing what they preached, the Gurus and their worthy disciples demonstrated that human life is worthless if not lived with honor and dignity. The 5th and the 9th Gurus, alongwith all four sons of the 10th Guru, and innumerable brave ones sacrificed their lives, at the altar of religious fanaticism, in order to uphold and preserve the liberty to practice a Faith of one's choice.

Heavenly-City : The fulfillment of the hopes of God's people for final salvation. To the ancient world cities represented ordered life, security from enemies, and material prosperity. See Cities and Urban Life. Hebrews says the city "has foundations;" its "architect and builder is God" (11:10 NASB); God has prepared it (11:16); and it is "the city of the living God, the heavenly Jerusalem" (12:22). This city is the home to "an innumerable company of angels" (12:22), to the assembly of the firstborn (12:23; an image of believers redeemed by the death of Christ; compare Ex. 13:13-15), and to the righteous made perfect by God (12:23; perhaps the Old Testament saints). Some interpreters take these descriptions literally. The Christian goal is, however, not something that can be touched and sensed like Israel's Sinai experience (12:18). Indeed, believers have already come (12:22) to the heavenly Jerusalem, at least in part.   Heaven is living in God's presence.

HELL The abode of the dead especially as a place of eternal punishment for unbelievers. Hell is an Anglo-Saxon word used to translate one Hebrew word and three Greek words in the King James Version of the Old and New Testaments. The Hebrew word that "hell" translated was *Sheol*. (Compare NASB). The word *Sheol* occurs sixty-five times in the Hebrew Bible. The King James Version translates thirty-one of the occurrences as "hell"; another thirty-one occurrences as "grave"; and three occurrences as "pit" (Num. 16:30, 33; Job 17:16). The Revised Standard Version never uses "hell" to translate *Sheol*. It does use "grave" one time as a translation of *Sheol* (Song of Sol. 8:6). It is experiencing virtual hell, being separated from God.

The existence of 'heaven' and/or 'hell', "per se", has been denied by the Sikh Gurus. They reject, outright, the school of thought that these are some 'designated areas', where a soul is dispatched, as per commendable deeds, or misdeeds.

Human ego ensnares one, thereby creating for the person 'heaven or hell'. Hankering after worldly pursuits, one creates hell for oneself [761 SGGS]

Wherever the saints reside, such a place reverberates with the ambience of heaven. They enshrine the Lotus Feet of God within their hearts. Listen, O mind and body, and recognize the way to find peace, so that you may eat and enjoy the various delicacies of the Lord. Taste the Ambrosial Nectar of the Naam, the Name of the Lord, within the mind. Its taste is wondrous — it cannot be described. All greed shall die, and all thirst shall be quenched. The humble beings seek the Sanctuary of the Supreme Lord God. The Lord dispels the fears and attachments of countless incarnations. God has showered His Mercy and Grace upon slave Nanak. [1142 SGGS]

Creating the Universe, God remains diffused throughout it. In the wind, water and fire, the Supreme is all pervasive. The waving mind seeks indulgence in evil passions and vices, forgetting its primal obligation towards the Creator. Forgetting God, one must be prepared to bear innumerable miseries. Consequently, such a misguided one suffers the ignominy of having to undergo 8.4 million reincarnations. This vicious cycle of death and rebirth has been termed as hell. Due to the present life misdeeds, one may be reborn as a four-legged animal, as a crawling serpent, as a flying bird, as a small insect or as a creature in water. In such dire straits, none from one's kith and kin shall be the savior; it is only within God power to rescue and redeem. Discard falsehood and attain the truth, and thus become the recipient of the rewards you desire. This, then, is the ideal and profitable bartering practice.[1028 SGGS]

Godliness: The whole of practical piety (1 Tim. 4:8; 2 Pet. 1:6). "It supposes knowledge, veneration, affection, dependence, submission, gratitude, and obedience."

In 1 Tim. 3:16 it denotes the substance of revealed religion.

Peace offerings : (Heb. *shelamim*), detailed regulations regarding given in Lev. 3; 7:11-21, 29-34. They were of three kinds

- (1.) Eucharist or thanksgiving offerings, expressive of gratitude for blessings received;
- (2.) in fulfillment of a vow, but expressive also of thanks for benefits received; and
- (3.) free-will offerings, something spontaneously devoted to God.

Good works are an expression of gratitude in the believer's heart (John 14:15, 23; Gal. 5:6). They are the fruits of the Spirit (Titus 2:10-12), and thus spring from grace, which they illustrate and strengthen in the heart.

Good works of the most sincere believers are all imperfect, yet like their persons they are accepted through the mediation of Jesus Christ (Col. 3:17), and so are rewarded; they have no merit intrinsically, but are rewarded wholly of grace.

One who forgets the Primal Lord, the Architect of karma, wanders around, tormented by the raging fires of desires. No one can save such an ungrateful person; he must suffer the terrors of the horrendous chambers of hell. He blessed us with the soul, the breath of life, the body and wealth; He preserved and nurtured us in our mother's womb. Forsaking His Love, we are entangled with duality; we shall never achieve our goals (of being happy).[1086 SGGS]

Forgetting Him, one's body turns to dust, and everyone calls him a ghost. And those, with whom he was deeply attached— they do not let him stay in their home, even for an instant. Practicing exploitation, he gathers wealth, but to what avail? As one sows, so does one reap; the body is the field of actions (karma). The ungrateful wretches forget the Lord, and wander in reincarnation. [706 SGGS]

They wear and eat the gifts from the Lord; how can they be so lazy and complacent, as to forget Him, O' mother? Forgetting her Husband Lord, and attaching herself to other affairs, the soul-bride foolishly discards the precious jewel in exchange for a mere shell. Human does not know the One who has bestowed these". [195 SGGS]

The sinner is unfaithful to himself; he is ignorant, with shallow understanding. He does not know the essence of all, the One who gave him body, soul and peace. In the illusionary lure of temptation, he goes out, searching in the ten directions. He does not enshrine the Generous Lord, the Great Giver, in his mind, even for an instant. Greed, falsehood, corruption and emotional attachment — these are what he stores, within his mind. [261 SGGS]

Sikhism lays great emphasis on being grateful to God, with every breath, while eating and walking, working and sleeping, throughout day and night, His reminiscence must pervade our thoughts, even subconsciously. One must, also, be grateful to fellow humans, for any favors received. Thanklessness has been denounced, vociferously.

The Lord looks upon us, and judges us, but the afflicted must be allowed the privilege of complaining; it is all the solace that such sorrow can find; and if in such distress words are spoken which should not be justified, yet the considerate and benevolent will hear them with indulgence. God is merciful;

He cast the tables out of his hands, and brake them—He might have done this through distress and anguish of spirit, on beholding their abominable idolatry and dissolute conduct; or he probably did it emblematically, intimating thereby that, as by this act of his the tables were broken in pieces, on which the law of God was written; so they, by their present conduct, had made a breach in the covenant, and broken the laws of their Maker. But we must not excuse this act; it was rash and irreverent; God's writing should not have been treated in this way.

"When the sun was going down, a deep sleep fell upon Abram; and behold, horror and great darkness fell upon him" (Genesis 15:12). Whenever God gives a vision to a Christian, it is as if He puts him in "the shadow of His hand" (Isaiah 49:2).

The saint's duty is to be still and listen. There is a "darkness" that comes from too much light—that is the time to listen. The story of Abram and Hagar in Genesis 16 is an excellent example of listening to so-called good advice during a time of darkness, rather than waiting for God to send the light. When God gives you a vision and darkness follows, wait. God will bring the vision He has given you to reality in your life if you will wait on His timing. Never try to help God fulfill His word. Abram went through thirteen years of silence, but in those years all of his self-sufficiency was destroyed.

Burning and burning, writhing in pain, one wrings one's hands, and goes insane. The Lord seems to be angry. The fault lies with the devotee, and not with the Lord. The devotee does not know His excellence and worth. Having wasted one's youth, now one comes to regret and repent. [794 SGGS]

When the people of the world are suffering in pain, they call upon the Lord in loving prayer. The True Lord naturally listens and hears and gives comfort. He commands the God of rain, and the rain pours down in torrents. Corn and wealth are produced in great abundance and prosperity; their value cannot be estimated. Sayeth Nanak : praise the Name of the Lord; He reaches out and sustains all beings. The mortal, never again, suffers in pain. [1281 SGGS]

In scientific-parlance, the 'Rotations & Revolutions', pertaining to the Earth and the Sun, bring about the change-of-seasons. It is a routine that is pre-programmed (in computer-jargon) in the characteristics of 'NATURE'. During scorching summers, the flow of rivers gets bogged down, while the same rivers get inundated, during rainy season. They dry out in summers, and submerge the entire region, when they are flooded. Vegetation cries out and birds and animals wail for a dewdrop and a raindrop, to quench their thirst. On hearing the pleas of the tormented souls, rains pour down, and flowers blossom, once again, and earth is rejuvenated.

Similarly, 'HEAT' is generated on the plane of the Mind & Soul, when desire, lust, anger, greed, attachment and other vices take their toll by vibrations and reverberations, attacking the human psyche. All the 'POSITIVES' have a cooling-effect on the human mind and body. Compassion and contentment, forgiveness and morality, along with other qualities of the head and the heart, forge a powerful alliance to counter the armies of aggressive elements (vices). Soothing signals emanate from such calm souls, and both, the sender and the receiver, experience 'BLISS'.

And thus it continues till the weaning of the child, or renewed pregnancy takes place. Here is a series of mercies and wise providential regulations which cannot be known without being admired, and which should be known that the great Creator and Preserver may have that praise from his creatures which his wonderful working demands.

And Moses blessed them—Gave them that praise which was due to their skill, diligence, and fidelity. See this meaning of the original word in the note on Genesis 2:3 (note). See also a fine instance of ancient courtesy between masters and their servants, in the case of Boaz and his reapers.
Thy father which seeth in secret—Let us not be afraid that our hearts can be concealed from God; but let us fear lest he perceive them to be more desirous of the praise of men than they are of that glory which comes from Him.

And ye shall know that I am the LORD your God—By thus fulfilling my promises ye shall know what is implied in my name. See Clarke's note on Exodus 6:3.

But why should God take such a most stupid, refractory, and totally worthless people for his people? 1. Because he had promised to do so to their noble ancestors Abraham, Isaac, Jacob, Joseph, Judah, etc., men worthy of all praise, because in general friends of God, devoted to his will and to the good of mankind.

Renounce both praise and criticism; seek, instead, the state of Nirvaana (Salvation). Says Nanak: this is such a difficult game; only those with faith in God understand it! [219 SGGS]

We have been burnt by the fires of the world. Some speak well of us, and some speak ill of us, but we have surrendered our body to God. Whoever comes to His Sanctuary, is saved by His Merciful Grace. Humble Nanak has entered His Sanctuary, Dear Lord, and pleads for the protection of his honor! [528 SGGS]

Even if one could live throughout the four ages, or even ten times more, and even if one were known throughout all the continents, and followed by all, with a good name and reputation, with praise and fame throughout the world—still, if the Lord does not bless one with His Glance of Grace, then who cares? What is the use? Among worms, one would be considered a lowly worm, and even contemptible sinners would hold one in contempt. [2 SGGS]

It is not good to slander anyone, but the foolish, self-willed still do it. The faces of the slanderers are blackened, and they fall into the most horrible hell. [755 SGGS]

Praise is an intoxicant, but self-aggrandizement is a Vice. When another praises one,, the former is, naturally, on cloud nine. Ironically, one does not like some one else being praised. This is the characteristic of a jealous mind. Criticism hurts, and it hurts all the more when someone, having the ulterior motive of defaming another, criticizes a noble and praise-worthy person. On the contrary, a sycophant (again, someone with a vested interest) would leave no stone unturned, to heap accolades and eulogies, on an undeserving person.

"The everlasting God ... neither faints nor is weary" (Isaiah 40:28).

Exhaustion means that our vital energies are completely worn out and spent. Spiritual exhaustion is never the result of sin, but of service. Whether or not you experience exhaustion will depend on where you get your supplies. Jesus said to Peter, "Feed My sheep," but He gave him nothing with which to feed them (John 21:17). The process of being made broken bread and poured-out wine means that *you* have to be the nourishment for other people's souls until they learn to feed on God. They must drain you completely —to the very last drop. But be careful to replenish your supply, or you will quickly be utterly exhausted. Until others learn to draw on the life of the Lord Jesus directly, they will have to draw on His life through you. You must literally be their source of supply, until they learn to take their nourishment from God. We owe it to God to be our best for His lambs and sheep, as well as for Him.

Have you delivered yourself over to exhaustion because of the way you have been serving God? If so, then renew and rekindle your desires and affections. Examine your reasons for service. Is your source based on your own understanding or is it grounded on the redemption of Jesus Christ? Continually look back to the foundation of your love and affection and remember where your Source of power lies. You have no right to complain, "O Lord, I am so exhausted." He saved and sanctified you to exhaust you. Be exhausted for God, but remember that He is your supply. "All my springs are in you" (Psalm 87:7).

Bowing down, and falling to the ground in humble prostration and adoration, countless times, before the All-powerful Lord. Plead for protection, to save one from wandering. God, reach out and give us Your Hand.[256 SGGS]

By Guru's Grace, one understands himself; know that, then, his negative desires are mollified/pacified (and his spiritual and worldly aspirations are fulfilled). In the Company of the Holy, one chants the Praises of the Lord. Such a devotee of the Lord is free of all disease. Night and day, sing the Holy hymns, the Praises of the One Lord. In the midst of one's household, remain balanced and unattached. One who places his hopes in the One Lord — the noose of Death is cut away from his neck. One whose mind hungers for the Supreme Lord, Says Nanak, shall not suffer pain. One who focuses his conscious mind on the Lord — that Saint is at peace; he does not waver. Those unto whom God has granted His Grace — who do those servants need to fear? As God is, so does He appear; in His Own creation, He Himself is pervading. Searching, tirelessly, the devotee achieves success, finally. [281 SGGS]

O soul, grasp the Support of the One Lord; give up all hopes in others, meditating on the Name of the Lord, your affairs shall be resolved. The mind's wanderings cease, when one comes to dwell in the Society of the Saints. If the Lord is Merciful from the very beginning, then one's mind is enlightened. Those who have the true wealth are the true bankers. The Lord, is their wealth, and they trade in His Name. Patience, glory and honor come to those who listen to the Name of the Lord. That God-loving person whose heart remains merged with the Lord, obtains glorious greatness. [257 SGGS]

Positive thoughts rejuvenate one's health: physical, mental, emotional and psychological. And, consequently, all of this has a notable impact on the person's total well being, and relationships, within the family, and in society, at large.

She is my sister—See the parallel account, Genesis 12 (note), and the notes there. Sarah was now about ninety years of age, and probably pregnant with Isaac. Her beauty, therefore, must have been considerably impaired since the time she was taken in a similar manner by Pharaoh, king of Egypt; but she was probably now chosen by Abimelech more on the account of forming an alliance with Abraham, who was very rich, than on account of any personal accomplishments. A petty king, such as Abimelech, would naturally be glad to form an alliance with such a powerful chief as Abraham was: we cannot but recollect his late defeat of the four confederate Canaanitish kings. See note on Genesis 14:14, etc. This circumstance was sufficient to establish his credit, and cause his friendship to be courted; and what more effectual means could Abimelech use in reference to this than the taking of Sarah, who he understood was Abraham's sister, to be his concubine or second wife, which in those times had no kind of disgrace attached to it?

Herodotus mentions a very singular custom among the Babylonians, which may serve to throw light on Laban's conduct towards Jacob. "In every district they annually assemble all the marriageable virgins on a certain day; and when the men are come together and stand round the place, the crier rising up sells one after another, always bringing forward the most beautiful first; and having sold her for a great sum of gold, he puts up her who is esteemed second in beauty. On this occasion the richest of the Babylonians used to contend for the fairest wife, and to outbid one another. But the vulgar are content to take the ugly and lame with money; for when all the beautiful virgins are sold, the crier orders the most deformed to stand up; and after he has openly demanded who will marry her with a small sum, she is at length given to the man that is contented to marry her with the least.

They alone are beautiful and attractive, who abide in the Company of the Holy. Those who have accumulated the wealth of the Lord's Name—they alone are wise investors, and are praised by all and sundry. [132 SGGS]

Power is fraudulent, beauty is fraudulent, and wealth is fraudulent, as is pride of ancestry. Beholding the bitter melon, he is deceived, by appearance. But it is not worth even a shell ; the illusionary riches will not go along with anyone.[708 SGGS]

"Beauty lies in the eyes of the beholder" is a realistically pertinent statement. And, equally true is the fact that Beauty, besides being external and physical, is, also, internal, intellectual and spiritual. To admire the latter, the observer must be endowed with the 'THIRD EYE' having the potential of penetrating through bone and flesh, to have the heavenly-view of the inner-beauty of someone's heart and soul. A living personification of this statement is the CRANE, exquisitely adorable, but so deceitful, inside. But, the ugly-looking Nightingale, which has been blessed with the most mellifluous voice, churning out soothing music (even while it may be the regular language of the species). Some beautiful people are treacherous and wicked and cunning, while the so-described ugly ones could be pious, learned and compassionate.

A child is showered with love and affection by all and sundry, owing to its qualities of beauty and innocence. It is free of the vices of greed, lust, malice, anger and ego. It is more carefree than the birds that fly in gay-abandon. The child-like traits are visible in God's chosen few, who continue to retain the charm and innocence, in word and spirit, until their last day. This Godly-attribute cannot be replenished and substituted by donning expensive ornaments and using cosmetics, to look beautiful. Saints, Seers, Saviours and Prophets, have a radiant gleam and glow on their faces, and a magnetic field and halo, around them, that would, instantaneously captivate anyone in range.

John 1: 5, 6.

Jesus told us that God is light and doesn't have any darkness in him. If we say that we share life with God and keep on living in the dark, we are lying and are not living by the truth. But if we live in the light, as God does, we share in life with each other.

Jesus said, "The words that I speak to you are spirit, and they are life" (John 6:63). Once, the Bible was just so many words to us—"clouds and darkness"—then, suddenly, the words become spirit and life because Jesus re-speaks them to us when our circumstances make the words new. That is the way God speaks to us; not by visions and dreams, but by words. When a man gets to God, it is by the simplest way—words. "Clouds and darkness surround Him ..." (Psalm 97:2).

"Whatever I tell you in the dark, speak in the light; and what you hear in the ear, preach on the housetops" (Matthew 10:27).

A person who has not been born again by the Spirit of God will tell you that the teachings of Jesus are simple. But when one is baptized by the Holy Spirit, one finds that "clouds and darkness surround him/her ... ." When we come into close contact with the teachings of Jesus Christ we have our first realization of this. The only possible way to have full understanding of the teachings of Jesus is through the light of the Spirit of God shining inside us. If we have never had the experience of taking our casual, religious shoes off our casual, religious feet—getting rid of all the excessive informality with which we approach God—it is questionable whether we have ever stood in His presence. Only after the amazing delight and liberty of realizing what Jesus Christ *does*, comes the impenetrable "darkness" of realizing who He is.

The Guru has provided the healing ointment of spiritual wisdom, and dispelled the darkness of ignorance. By the lord's Grace, one meets the Saint; sayeth Nanak : "My mind has been enlightened". [293 SGGS]

If a hundred moons were to rise, and a thousand suns appeared, even with such light, there would still be terrifying darkness (in the mind), without the Guru's guidance. Says Nanak : those who do not think of the Guru, and who think of themselves as clever, shall be left abandoned in the field, like the scattered sesame.[463 SGGS]

Darkness is to be found all over, and in great measure, within man's mind, and without. The earth's crust is dark, towards the interior. The deeper levels of the oceans are dark, the sun's light being unable to permeate, beyond a specified range (fathoms). Due to the increased effect of the vices of Lust, Greed, Egocentricism, Hatred, Jealousy, Violence and Addictions, even more darkness can be found within the hearts and minds and souls of the modern human.

The germs of disease originate in dark regions. Snakes and scorpions are often found in dark areas. Dacoits and marauders wait for their preys, in dark and nether confines. And, so do the lowly vices wait for the opportune moment to launch a vicious attack targeted towards persons with a weak power of resilience. 'Darkness' is a synonym for 'sorrow', 'grief' and 'penury'. And ostentatious illuminations and fireworks are on display, during festivities and rejoicing. Due to the darkness of ignorance, coupled with a lack of will and interest, to search and pray for the True Light, today's man is lost and frightened. Finding oneself in deep peril, there seems to be no happiness, notwithstanding the rapid strides towards the destinations of acquiring material-wealth and accruing knowledge.

Luke 6: 39, 40.

Asks Jesus: "Can one blind person lead another blind person ? Won't they both fall into a ditch ? Are students better than their teacher ? But, when they are fully trained they will be like their teacher".

Your heavenly Father knoweth, etc.—The sixth reason against this anxiety about the future is—because God, our heavenly Father, is infinite in wisdom, and knows all our wants. It is the property of a wise and tender father to provide necessaries, and not superfluities, for his children. Not to expect the former is an offense to his goodness; to expect the latter is injurious to his wisdom.

I will liken him unto a wise man—To a prudent man, a man of sense and understanding, who, foreseeing the evil hideth himself, who proposes to himself the best end, and makes use of the proper means to accomplish it. True wisdom consists in getting the building of our salvation completed: to this end we must build on the Rock, CHRIST JESUS, and make the building firm, by keeping close to the maxims of his Gospel, and having our tempers and lives conformed to its word and spirit; and when, in order to this, we lean on nothing but the grace of Christ, we then build upon a solid rock. The words of my roaring? The Vulgate, Septuagint, Syriac, Ethiopic, and Arabic, with the Anglo-Saxon, make use of terms, which may be thus translated: "My sins (or foolishness) are the cause why deliverance is so far from me." It appears that these versions have read "my sin of ignorance," instead of "my roaring:" but no MS. extant supports this reading.

FOOL AND FOLLY Translations of several uncomplimentary words which appear approximately 360 times throughout the Old and New Testaments to describe unwise and ungodly people. The words are especially predominant in the Wisdom Literature of the Old Testament. Persons who do not possess wisdom are called "fools".

A person performing a misdeed, fully well aware and conscious of the repercussions, thereof, and realizing the fallout, is deemed to be the greatest fool. Instead of feeling guilt or remorse, he becomes arrogant and egocentric, and takes pride in his actions. He is like the one who falls into a well, despite carrying a glowing lamp, with him. [1376 SGGS]

GOD gave humans the unique gift of the power of analysis, and by the optimum utilization of the nervous system (the brain), one could achieve wonders. But, rarely, does that happen. A child's thinking faculties are not fully developed, hence cannot be called a fool. But, such an adult is a fool, who does not think and act rationally. A person lacking in wisdom, does not act in consonance with certain universally acclaimed and socially acceptable norms.

A literate or educated person may not, necessarily, be a wise one, too. But, God may gift an illiterate person with the blessing of wisdom. And, there's no guarantee that an educated person would realize God, while there have been great devotees, who never learnt the Three "Rs" in school, but mastered the highest techniques of Communion with God. Another MYTH and ill-conceived notion pertains to the prevalent practice of linking intelligence and wisdom with wealth and prestige. A person who is successful in a given vocation/profession might not, necessarily, be considered wise, in other spheres, too. But, generally, there is a tendency to become dependant, upon such people, in various matters, including Spiritual-Religious and Socio-economic, even though the concerned person might not be, remotely, having an affinity with the said issues.

Thy will be done—This petition is properly added to the preceding; for when the kingdom of righteousness, peace, and joy, in the Holy Spirit, is established in the heart, there is then an ample provision made for the fulfillment of the Divine will.

The will of God is infinitely good, wise, and holy; to have it fulfilled in and among men, is to have infinite goodness, wisdom, and holiness diffused throughout the universe; and earth made the counterpart of heaven.

Behold, I bring you good tidings—I am not come to declare the judgments of the Lord, but his merciful loving-kindness, the subject being a matter of great joy. He then declares his message. Unto you—to the Jews first, and then to the human race. Some modern MSS. with the utmost impropriety read ἡμῖν, us, as if angels were included in this glorious work of redemption; but St. Paul says, he took not upon him the nature of angels, but the seed of Abraham, i.e. the nature of Abraham and his posterity, the human nature; therefore the good news is to you,—and not to yourselves exclusively, for it is to all people, to all the inhabitants of this land, and to the inhabitants of the whole earth.

She called his name Ben-oni—the Son of my sorrow or affliction, because of the hard labor she had in bringing him into the world; but his father called him Benjamin, the son of my right hand, i.e., the son peculiarly dear to me. So man of the right hand, Psalm 80:17, signifies one much loved and regarded of God. The Samaritan has Benyamin, the son of days; i.e., the son of his old age, as Judah calls him, Genesis 44:20; and Houbigant contends that this is the true reading, and that the Chaldee termination is a corruption. If it were a corruption, it is as old as the days of St. Jerome, who translated the place Benjamin, that is, the son of the right hand.

127

*One who understands the essence of a 'Life-Divine', such a humble
one (ever in God's servitude) is very rare. He has, not even, an iota of
pain, and is, totally, at peace. There is no defeat — he is totally
victorious. He is never in sorrow — he is happy, always. Says
Nanak: the humble servant of the Lord is himself the Lord (becomes
identical; resembles Godly-Attributes); he does not come and go in the
vicious cycle of reincarnation.[1302 SGGS]*

Sorrow and pain is like an epidemic, the only cure for it being the
regular administering of dosages of Noumenon of God. None has
escaped the octopus-like tentacles of sorrow. Since the desires are
innumerable, the causes of sorrow are countless, too. When desires
are not fulfilled, pain is born, therefrom.

*In hope, there is very great pain; the self-willed focuses his
consciousness on it. The God-loving become desire less, and attain
supreme peace. In the midst of their household, they remain detached;
Sorrow and separation do not cling to them at all. They are pleased
with the Lord's Will. Says Nanak, they remain forever immersed in the
Primal Lord, who blends them with Himself. [1249 SGGS]*

It is human nature to be jealous of another's happiness, and to cry
hoarse at one's own sorrow. But, in reality, NONE is actually happy,
in this world. The nodal-point and focus of all happiness (the reservoir
of Joy and Bliss) is GOD and meditation on His Name. Every laughter
is attached with the apprehension of a wail looming large. And behind
the curtain of all praise and accolades, lurks the dangerous snake of
exposure, insult and defamation. Profits are, naturally, made, at great
stakes and risks. Hence, all efforts should be made to decorate this life
with all worthy attributes and ornamentation, so as to be received by
God, in His Magnificent Kingdom, with Honor and Praise. At that
moment, disgrace and rebuke can be avoided, if one had the wisdom,
of doing so, during the time that was available, for meditation, during
the lifetime.

Of alms giving, Math.vv. 1-5. Of prayer, vv. 6-8. The Lord's prayer, or model according to which Christians should pray, vv. 9-13. Of forgiveness, vv. 14, 15. Of fasting, vv. 16, 17. Of laying up treasures, vv. 18-21. Of the single eye, vv. 22, 23. The impossibility of serving two masters, v. 24. Of contentment and confidence in the Divine providence, vv. 25-32. Directions about seeking the kingdom of God, vv. 33, 34.

CONTENTMENT An internal satisfaction which does not demand changes in external circumstances. The New Testament expresses this with the Greek word *arkew* and its derivatives. Hebrews 13:15 summarizes the teaching in advising believers to be free of the love of money and to depend on God's promise not to forsake His people. Food and lodging should be enough for the godly (1 Tim. 6:6-10; compare Matt. 6:34; contrast Luke 12:19). The believer can be content no matter what the outward circumstances (Phil. 4:11-13). Believers are content to know the Father (John 14:8-9) and depend on His grace (2 Cor. 12:9-10; compare 2 Cor. 9:8-11).

GREED An excessive or reprehensible desire to acquire; covetousness. The greed of Eli's sons for the best part of the sacrifices disqualified them from the priesthood (1 Sam. 2:29). Hosea condemned priests who were greedy for the people's iniquity (4:8 NRSV), that is, greedy for the sin offerings.

Jesus warned against all types of greed (Luke 12:15; KJV covetousness). The Pauline standard for Christian ministry gave no pretext for greed (1 Thess. 2:5; 1 Tim 3:3, 8). Greed marked the Gentile or pagan way of life (Eph. 4:19).

The greed of *Gehazi* in asking Naaman for some of the rich gifts that Elisha had refused to accept was met by his being cursed with Naaman's *leprosy*.

What good is food, and what good are attires & adornments, if the True Lord does not abide within the mind? What good are fruits, what good is butter, what good is sweet molasses, and what good is flour? What good are clothes, and what good is a soft bed, to enjoy pleasures and sensual delights? What good is an army, and what good are soldiers, servants and mansions to live in? Says Nanak : without the True Name, all this paraphernalia is perishable.[142 SGGS]

Nanak wonders : what has happened to the world? There is no guide or friend. There is no love, even among brothers and relatives. For the sake of worldly riches, people have lost their faith. They weep and wail. They slap their faces and pull their hair out. But if they chant the Name of the Lord, they shall be absorbed into it.[1410 SGGS]

GREED is considered to be a major vice that leads one onto other dangerous vices like violence and deceit. It assumes the proportions of a mental disease, when in reaches the saturation point.

The natural equilibrium is disturbed, when a greedy person accumulates immense wealth, while another person has to shiver in the cold, shelter less, sans clothing.

To remain happy with whatsoever one has, is True Contentment. This should not be misconstrued to imply that being ambitious is negative, provided the rapid strides towards success DO NOT, in any way, impinge upon another's interests. Abundance of wealth and materials does not guarantee happiness. Peace is the direct consequence of Contentment. Being progressive is welcome, without usurping another's rights and privileges.

Practices and emotions associated with the experience of the death of a loved one or of other catastrophe or tragedy. The Bible tells us of life and death. When it mentions death, the Bible frequently relates the experience of the participants. So we are told of the mourning of Abraham for Sarah (Gen. 23:2). Jacob mourned for Joseph, thinking he was dead. "and Jacob rent his clothes, and put sackcloth upon his loins, and mourned for his son many days ... he refused to be comforted; and he said, For I will go down into the grave unto my son mourning. Thus his father wept for him" (Gen. 37:34-35). The Egyptians mourned for Jacob 70 days (Gen. 50:3).

David led the people as they mourned Abner (2 Sam. 3:31-32).

Mary and Martha wept over their brother Lazarus (John 11:31). After Jesus watched Mary and her friends weeping, we are told, "Jesus wept" (John 11:35). Mourning was expressed in three major ways: Weeping was then, as now, the primary indication of grief. Tears are repeatedly mentioned, "My tears have been my meat day and night" (Ps. 42:3a). "Thou tellest my wanderings: put thou my tears into thy bottle" (Ps. 56:8a). We have already noted Mary's tears and even those of Jesus. The loud lamentation was also a feature of mourning.

That state of continual sanctification, that life of purity and detachment from the world and all its lusts, without which detachment and sanctity no man shall see the Lord—shall never enjoy his presence in the world of blessedness. To see God, in the Hebrew phrase, is to enjoy him; and without holiness of heart and life this is impossible. No soul can be fit for heaven that has not suitable dispositions for the place. Consider the state of grace in which you once stood; the happiness, love, and joy which you felt when ye received remission of sins;

Where is that door, where You live, O Lord? What is that door called?
Among all doors, who can find that door? For the sake of that door,
one wanders around sadly, detached from the world; [877 SGGS]
Having no anxiety about dying, and nurturing no hope of living. You
are the Cherisher of all beings.[20 SGGS]

One observes no difference between Optimism & Pessimism, in a state
of Real Detachment. The literal meaning (of detachment) would be,
being in a state of utter despair, sadness, even to the extreme of
becoming a recluse. But, the deeper, philosophic implication, in the
context of spiritual -realms, would be: being with oneself, in solitude,
with courage-of-conviction, and fortitude, in a contemplative and
meditative state . Now, this frame-of- mind, and unique level could be
attained even while one is sitting in a vast multitude of people, and yet
calm and composed, within.. Talking, working, eating or whatever, but
the thought is concentrated on the "ONLY ONE".

Under varying circumstances, the individual would, obviously react
differently. In the event of the loss of a dear one, the bereaved
relations of the deceased are naturally saddened. Similarly, a person
afflicted   with   physical-ailments,   financial-losses,
emotional/psychological traumas, might, even, start thinking in terms
of committing self-immolation/suicide.

This, then, could be described as a FATAL DETACHMENT, born out
of disenchantment/disillusionment with life. This would be the direct
consequence of a lack or absence of spiritual temper, and faith in God.
It is developed, gradually, depending upon the intensity of the
distinctly varied experiences one has had. On the contrary, on attaining
pristine knowledge, one becomes desirous of detachment, even while
not foregoing worldly -existence and life. Life, now, seems as if it
were a bubble of air, on the surface of water, waiting to burst any
moment.

Old Testament Teaching In the Old Testament, "freedom" is used to describe what God desires and grants to Hebrew slaves. According to the law, no person is to have complete mastery of another. Consequently, the Law stipulates that a person can only be used as a slave for six years. Even so, if they are mistreated during that time, they are to be released. Also, every fifty years, all slaves are to be freed, regardless of how many years of their slavery they have served (Ex. 21:2-11, 26, 27; Lev. 25:10; Deut. 15:12-18). In the example of the Exodus and the preaching of the prophets, whoever is oppressed is viewed as a slave, and God desires that the oppression stop. He not only makes it the task of His people to stop oppression, but even says that if they don't, He will do it Himself (Isa. 58:6; 61:1, Jer. 34)

Throughout the Old Testament, freedom is predominantly used to express control over the physical circumstances of life. By the time of the New Testament, it was widely recognized that no persons are free to such an extent that they have control of their physical circumstances. Even the rich are subject to war, drought, and other calamities. Nevertheless, an influential group called Stoics believed that anyone could still attain true freedom, because no person or force of nature can control the inner life. Thus, the individual is ultimately in control of self, though not of the environment.

The Hebrew women are not as the Egyptian women—This is a simple statement of what general experience shows to be a fact, viz., that women, who during the whole of their pregnancy are accustomed to hard labor, especially in the open air, have comparatively little pain in parturition. At this time the whole Hebrew nation, men and women, were in a state of slavery, and were obliged to work in mortar and brick, and all manner of service IN THE FIELD, Exodus 1:14.

Now, the Merciful Lord hath decreed that nobody shall persecute and torture another, and that all may reside in peace and harmony, under His Benevolent Rule. [74 SGGS]

Fareed implores the Lord, not to let him live on alms, and on another's mercy. Instead, he would prefer death, to slavery.[1380 SGGS]

The battle-drums and conch-shells signal the commencement of the battle. The spiritual warriors enter the battle-field, in all their paraphernalia and regalia. He alone is known as a spiritual hero, who fights in defense of religion (NOT the religions or faiths that we have founded, BUT the religion of the Lord : that wants us to sacrifice our lives for peace and justice, and to never let cowardice devour us). He may be cut apart, limb by limb, but he never withdraws from the war-zone. [1105 SGGS]

The God-loving and the God-fearing warriors would never subjugate another, but would use their power to protect the weak and the downtrodden, the oppressed and the suppressed. Freedom is the birthright of every human, while slavery is a curse. In this context, it is noteworthy that the Sikh people have been, relentlessly, carrying on an agitation, demanding a separate homeland, as promised by the lawmakers of free India, at the time of framing the Constitution of India, at the end of the imperialistic colonial rule of the British, who created Pakistan, on religious lines, as an Islamic State.

Most recently, in 1984 when the Indian regime launched a war-like operation to attack the holiest Sikh shrine, The Golden Temple, the Sikhs have been constantly persecuted, dubbed as extremists, killed in fake police and army encounters, and jailed without free-trial, for several years, on end. The Sikhs have been waging a struggle for freedom, due to the Spirit of Freedom, that was inculcated in them by all Gurus.

Section 4

BEWARE

The 'negative forces' have played havoc with
humanity: whether it is religious fanaticism or
superstition, whether ritualistic superficiality
or discrimination on account of race, color,
status, caste.
Then, there are the addictions and vices,
Struggle for power and supremacy,
plunging humanity in to the darkest dungeons
of ignorance and cruelty.
This lowly existence was not what
God intended for us, giving us the
'gift of brain', to distinguish between
right and wrong, good and evil.

"Lift up your eyes on high, and see who has created these things ..." (Isaiah 40:26).

The people of God in Isaiah's time had blinded their minds' ability to see God by looking on the face of idols. But Isaiah made them look up at the heavens; that is, he made them begin to use their power to think and to visualize correctly. If we are children of God, we have a tremendous treasure in nature and will realize that it is holy and sacred. We will see God reaching out to us in every wind that blows, every sunrise and sunset, every cloud in the sky, every flower that blooms, and every leaf that fades, if we will only begin to use our blinded thinking to visualize it; rather, it is not as much a matter of visualizing it, as much as opening our eyes to see reality apart from the blindness of our false ways of thinking.

The real test of spiritual focus is being able to bring your mind and thoughts under control. Is your mind focused on the face of an idol? Is the idol you? Is it your work? Is it your idea of what a servant should be, or maybe your experience of salvation and sanctification? If so, then your ability to see God is blinded. You will be powerless when faced with difficulties and will be forced to endure in darkness. If your power to see has been blinded, don't look back on your own experiences, but look to God. It is God you need. Go beyond yourself and away from the faces of your idols and away from everything else that has been blinding your thinking. Wake up and accept the ridicule that Isaiah gave to his people, and deliberately turn your thoughts and your eyes to God.

One of the reasons for our sense of futility in prayer is that we have lost our power to visualize. We can no longer even imagine putting ourselves deliberately before God. It is actually more important to be broken bread and poured-out wine in the area of intercession.

Illusion & Superstition are such horrific banes that have clutched humanity in their tentacles; one who is not controlled by these 'diseases' finds peace and joy.

The egg of doubt has burst; and the mind has been enlightened. The Guru has shattered the shackles on the feet, and has set the devotee free, released from the bondage, and from the vicious cycle of reincarnation. The boiling cauldron has cooled down; the Guru has blessed the devotee with the cooling, soothing Name of the Lord. The devotee has made Truth his life's purpose. True is the capital, and True is the merchandise. One may practice intensive meditation, and discipline his body, but his mind still runs around in ten directions. The celibate practices celibacy, but his heart is filled with pride. The renunciate wanders around at sacred shrines of pilgrimage, but his mindless anger is still within him. Others go on fasts, take vows, perform the six rituals and wear religious robes, to brag about. Some sing songs and melodies and hymns, but their minds do not sing the praise of the Lord. Says Nanak, "I met the Perfect Guru, and then the anxiety of my mind was removed. The Beloved of my soul knows everything; all trivial talk is forgotten".[1002 SGGS]

People are entangled in myriad forms of enjoyment: clothes, perfumes, gold and diamonds, food and drinks, merry-making and dancing, horses and elephants, mansions and palaces, adultery and gambling, realizing not that all of these constitute dust, just as the human body, itself. [42 SGGS]

This world is an illusion, where people pass their lives, in a deep slumber (forgetting that they are here as 'guests', not as the owners of the 'home' they occupy). [36 SGGS]

The many forms of Illusionary-Hallucinations shall, surely, pass away, eventually; know that they are, all, transitory.[268 SGGS]

The Disputation of Nebridius Against the Manichaeans, on the Question "Whether God Be Corruptible or Incorruptible."

It was enough for me, Lord, to oppose to those deceived deceivers, and dumb praters, since Thy word sounded not out of them; that was enough which long ago, while we were yet at Carthage, Nebridius used to propound, at which all we that heard it were staggered: "That said nation of darkness, which the Manichees are wont to set as an opposing mass over against Thee, what could it have done unto Thee, hadst Thou refused to fight with it? For, if they answered, 'it would have done Thee some hurt,' then shouldest Thou be subject to injury and corruption:

Woe to the prosperities of the world, once and again, through fear of adversity, and corruption of joy! Woe to the adversities of the world, once and again, and the third time, from the longing for prosperity, and because adversity itself is a hard thing, and lest it shatter endurance. Is not the life of man upon earth all trial: without any interval?

For corruption injures, but unless it diminished goodness, it could not injure. Either then corruption injures not, which cannot be; or which is most certain, all which is corrupted is deprived of good.

And Thou knowest how far Thou hast already changed me, who first healedst me of the lust of vindicating myself, that so Thou mightest forgive all the rest of my iniquities, and heal all my infirmities, and redeem life from corruption, and crown me with mercy and pity, and satisfy my desire with good things: who didst curb my pride with Thy fear, and tame my neck to Thy yoke. And now I bear it and it is light unto me, because so hast Thou promised, and hast made it; and verily so it was, and I knew it not, when I feared to take it.

The self-willed egoistic persons read and study, but they do not know the way. They do not understand the Name of the Lord; they wander, deluded and deluged by doubt. They take bribes, and give false testimony; the noose of evil-mindedness is around their necks, and they shall hang themselves. They read the Scriptures; they argue and debate, but do not know the essence of reality; they indulge in rituals and ceremonial practices. Without the Perfect Guru, the essence of reality is not obtained. The true and pure beings walk the Path of Truth. He Himself is wise, and He Himself judges the Truth. Those whom God blesses with His Glance of Grace become God-loving, and praise the Word of the Holy hymns. [1032 SGGS]

One who usurps the rights of others, oppresses and expoloits the weak, in effect disgraces his own religious belief, and commits a horrendous sin. [141 SGGS]

Such actions/deeds are severely deplorable, and tantamount to a grave SIN. Feeding one's children, from the money gotten through corrupt means, is just like poisoning their food, with the venom of a snake. A person whose intake is such, shall have vitriolic speech and a foul tongue, never pleasant in conversation and in his dealings with others.

Such misdemeanors of the corrupt do not go unpunished. They shall be penalized, on earth, and in God's Supreme Court.

How Could Someone So Persecute Jesus!

"Saul, Saul, why are you persecuting me?" (Acts 26:14).

Are you determined to have your own way in living for God? We will never be free from this trap until we are brought into the experience of the baptism of "the Holy Spirit and fire" (Matthew 3:11). Stubbornness and self-will will always stab Jesus Christ. It may hurt no one else, but it wounds His Spirit. Whenever we are obstinate and self-willed and set on our own ambitions, we are hurting Jesus. Every time we stand on our own rights and insist that this is what we intend to do, we are persecuting Him. Whenever we rely on self-respect, we systematically disturb and grieve His Spirit. And when we finally understand that it is Jesus we have been persecuting all this time, it is the most crushing revelation ever.

Is the Word of God tremendously penetrating and sharp in me as I hand it on to you, or does my life betray the things I profess to teach? I may teach sanctification and yet exhibit the spirit of Satan, the very spirit that persecutes Jesus Christ. The Spirit of Jesus is conscious of only one thing—a perfect oneness with the Father. And He tells us, "Take My yoke upon you and learn from Me, for I am gentle and lowly in heart, and you will find rest for your souls" (Matthew 11:29). All I do should be based on a perfect oneness with Him, not on a self-willed determination to be godly. This will mean that others may use me, go around me, or completely ignore me, but if I will submit to it for His sake, I will prevent Jesus Christ from being persecuted.

One has not forsaken sexual desire, and not forgotten anger; greed has not departed, either. There's no stop to slandering and gossiping about others. All service is useless and fruitless. By breaking into the houses of others and robbing them, one fills one's belly, what a sinner. But, when this sinner goes to the world beyond, he shall be notorious, for all his acts of omission and commission, that he hath committed, due to ignorance. Cruelty has not left his mind; he has not cherished kindness for other living beings.[1253 SGGS]

When oppression and tyranny are on the ascendant, a myriad array of vices controls the human-frame (body and mind). The bondage of self-aggrandizement can be gotten rid of by meditating upon God's Name. That's the only remedy for the tormented oppressor as well as the weak and cowardly oppressed.[255 SGGS]

The emperor who struck down the poor, has been burnt in the fire by the Supreme Lord God. The Creator administers true justice. He is the Saving Grace of His slaves. [199 SGGS]

It is tyranny to use force; the Lord shall call the cruel to account. And then they shall be tortured and humiliated, in the Lord's Court. Keep the slate of conscience clean and clear, to become the recipient of God's Grace. Only then, in the True Court of the Lord, one shall not be captured or put in shackles. [1375 SGGS]

It is not said, Confess your faults to the ELDERS that they may forgive them, or prescribe penance in order to forgive them. No; the members of the Church were to confess their faults to each other; therefore auricular confession to a priest, such as is prescribed by the Romish Church, has no foundation in this passage. Indeed, had it any foundation here it would prove more than they wish, for it would require the priest to confess his sins to the people, as well as the people to confess theirs to the priest.

The purpose and intent of a making a voluntary confession is to request for, in all humility and submission, forgiveness from the entire Congregation/community/society.　When we sin, we hurt ALL, collectively; it is, therefore, that the priest grants pardon to the sinner, in the name of all those whose rights the sinner has transgressed.

And pray one for another—There is no instance in auricular confession where the penitent and the priest pray together for pardon; but here the people are commanded to pray for each other that they may be healed.

Sacrifice　The OT writers saw sacrifice as a means which God had given men to enable them to have fellowship with him. The fundamental underlying belief was the idea of the covenant. In essence, sacrifice was always a prayer to which was added the idea of giving, of real offering. Other elements mingled with this. First, there was the search for a sure and exclusive relationship with God through blood. Then sacrifice became an accepted way of averting punishment, a sort of penance. Finally, there came the idea of atonement effected by a restitution sacrifice.

The man of false mind practices falsehood. He runs after illusion, and yet pretends to be a man of disciplined meditation. Deluded by doubt, he visits all the sacred shrines of pilgrimage. How can such a man of disciplined meditation attain the supreme status? By Guru's Grace, one lives the Truth. Nanak declares that such a man of disciplined meditation attains liberation. He alone is a man of disciplined meditation, who practices this self-discipline. Meeting with the True Guru, he contemplates the Word of the Holy hymns. Such a man of disciplined meditation is honored in the Court of the Lord. [948 SGGS]

Service to the Guru is the greatest sublime penance. The Dear Lord dwells in the mind, and all suffering departs. Then, at the Gate of the True Lord, one appears truthful. Serving the Guru, one comes to know the three worlds. Understanding his own self, he obtains the Lord. How very fortunate are they, who are committed to the Guru's service. Night and day, they are engaged in devotional worship; the True Name is implanted within them. Nanak chants the true thought. Keep the Name of the Lord enshrined within your heart. Imbued with devotion to the Lord, the gate of salvation is found.[423 SGGS]

Do not heat the body like a furnace, or burn your bones like firewood. What wrong have your head and feet done to deserve such a punitive action? See the Husband Lord within. God, the Cosmic Husband dwells within all hearts; without Him, there is no heart at all. Says Nanak : Such Devotees are the happy, virtuous soul-brides; the Lord is close to them.[1411 SGGS]

Please note : **'PENANCE' & 'REPENTANCE'** have been listed under the NEGATIVE-INFLUENCES, because they arise out of another negative feeling : GUILT.

Atonement and the Cross The focal point of God's atoning work is Christ's death on the cross. Paul wrote that "when we were enemies, we were reconciled to God by the death of his Son" (Rom. 5:10). These words not only define the meaning of atonement, they reveal the heart of the gospel as well.

Though atonement is focused in the cross, the New Testament makes clear that Christ's death is the climax of His perfect obedience. He "became obedient unto death, even the death of the cross" (Phil. 2:8). "Though he were a Son, yet learned he obedience by the things which He suffered" (Heb. 5:8). Romans 5:12-19 contrasts Christ's obedience with Adam's disobedience. His sinless obedience qualified Him to be the perfect Sacrifice for sin (Heb. 6:8-10).

Furthermore, the New Testament interprets the cross in light of the resurrection. Atonement is the achievement of Christ crucified and risen. So important is this emphasis that Paul affirms, "and if Christ be not raised, your faith is vain; ye are yet in your sins" (1 Cor. 15:17).

The Necessity of Atonement The necessity for Christ's atoning work is occasioned by the breach in the relationship between the Creator and the creature. This breach is the result of humanity's sinful rebellion. "But your iniquities have separated between you and your God, and your sins have hid his face from you, that he will not hear" (Isa. 59:2). Thus, in their unreconciled state people are God's "enemies" (Rom. 5:10), have "enmity against God" (Rom. 8:7), and have "no hope" (Eph. 2:12). There is no difference between Jew and Gentile in this respect, "for all have sinned and come short of the glory of God" (Rom. 3:23).

Twelve years pass in childhood, and for another twenty years, he does not practice self-discipline and austerity. For another thirty years, he does not worship God in any way, and then, when he is old, he repents and regrets. His life is wasted, in greed and egoistic pride. He is powerless. He makes a dam around the dried-up pool (of his power), and he makes a fence around the harvested field, but when the thief of Death comes, he quickly carries away what the fool had tried to preserve as his own. His feet and head and hands begin to tremble, and the tears flow copiously from his eyes. His tongue has not spoken the correct words, but now, he hopes to practice religion! If the Dear Lord shows His Mercy, even a sinner would earn the Profit of the Lord's Name. By Guru's Grace, he receives the wealth of the Lord's Name, which alone shall go with him, when he departs. Says Kabeer : listen, O Saints — he shall not take any other wealth with him. When the summons comes from the King, the Lord of the Universe, the mortal departs, leaving behind his wealth and mansions. 479 SGGS]

Now, how does one tackle this situation and find appropriate remedies? What efforts should one make? How can one dispel the anxieties of one's mind? How can one be ferried across these turbulent seas? Obtaining this human incarnation, one has done no good deeds; this makes him very frightened. In thought, word and deed, one has not sung the Lord's Praises; this thought torments the mind. He listened to the Guru's Teachings, but spiritual wisdom did not well up within him; like a beast, he filled his belly. Says Nanak : "O God, please confirm Your Law of Grace; for only then can a sinner be saved".[685 SGGS]

146

Luke 6: 27, 28, 29 ; Matthew 5.38-48; 7.12a

Love your enemies, and be good to everyone who hates you. Ask God to bless anyone who curses you, and pray for everyone who is cruel to you. If someone slaps you on one cheek, don't stop that person from slapping you on the other cheek. If someone tries to take your coat, don't try to keep back your shirt".

ENVY A painful or resentful awareness of another's advantage joined with the desire to possess the same advantage. The advantage may concern material goods (Gen. 26:14) or social status (30:1). Old Testament wisdom frequently warns against envying the arrogant (Ps. 73:3), the violent (Prov. 3:31), or the wicked (Ps. 37:1; Prov. 24:1, 19). In the New Testament envy is a common member of vice lists as that which comes out of the person and defiles (Mark 7:22), as a characteristic of humanity in rebellion to God (Rom. 1:29), as a fruit of the flesh (Gal. 5:21), as a characteristic of unregenerate life (Tit. 3:3) and as a trait of false teachers (1 Tim. 6:4). Envy (sometimes translated jealousy by modern translations) was the motive leading to the arrest of Jesus (Matt. 27:18; Mark 15:10) and to opposition to the gospel in Acts (Acts 5:17, 13:45; 17:5). Christians are called to avoid envy (Gal. 5:26; 1 Pet. 2:1).

Envy is sometimes a motive for doing good. The Preacher was disillusioned that hard work and skill were the result of envying another (Eccl. 4:4). Paul was, however, able to rejoice that the gospel was preached even if the motive were envy (Phil. 1:15). Contrary to modern translations, the Greek word used for envy here (phthonos) is always used in a negative sense, never in the positive sense of God's jealousy (Greek zealos). God's response to the sinful longings of the human heart is to give more grace (4:6).

Do not harbor hatred against anyone. In each and every heart, God is contained. The All-pervading Lord is permeating and pervading the oceans and the land. How rare are those who, by Guru's Grace, sing of Him. Hatred and alienation depart from those who, as devotees, listen to the Hymns of the Lord's Praises. Says Nanak : one who becomes a devotee chants the Name of the Lord, and rises above all social classes and status symbols. Acting in egotism, selfishness and conceit, the foolish, ignorant, faithless cynic wastes his life. He dies in agony, like one dying of thirst.[259 SGGS]

To some, the Lord has given silks and satins, and to some, beds decorated with cotton ribbons. Some do not even have a poor patched coat, and some live in thatched huts. Do not indulge in envy and bickering, O my mind. By continually performing good deeds, O my mind, you may have the luxuries, but not through jealousy. The potter works with the same clay, and colors the pots in different ways. Into some, he sets pearls (of contentment and compassion), while to others, he attaches filth (of hatred, and an envious nature).[479 SGGS]

Harbouring animosity towards our fellow human beings is tantamount to perpetrating violence on our own soul. It's like raising a banner of revolt against God and his offspring. And, as all of us are HIS children, it is inferred that its equivalent to fighting with our own siblings, rebelling against our own kith and kin.

Beware lest any man spoil you through philosophy and vain deceit, after the tradition of men, after the rudiments of the world, and not after Christ. For in Him dwelleth all the fulness of the Godhead bodily (Col. 2:8:9)

And since at that time (Thou, O light of my heart, knowest) Apostolic Scripture was not known to me, I was delighted with that exhortation, so far only, that I was thereby strongly roused, and kindled, and inflamed to love, and seek, and obtain, and hold, and embrace not this or that sect, but wisdom itself whatever it were; and this alone checked me thus unkindled, that the name of Christ was not in it.

The people of Gibeon, just six miles from Bethel, were the only inhabitants of the land who pursued means of peace. Gibeon was a royal city, greater than Ai and the largest city of the Hivites. Located in the central part of the country, they held a strategic place for invasion against the Israelites. Rather than join the confederacy, the people of Gibeon chose to seek a peace pact with Israel. They sought peace though in what would be considered a very strange, or as the Scripture put it, "wilily" manner. It was crafty and deceitful, but we are reminded of the circumstances with Rahab in Joshua 2, when she acted on the basis of deceit. These characteristics are a way of life with people who live in heathenism. Here the Gibeonites acted on knowledge of what God had done on behalf of the children of Israel (Joshua 9:9). They had knowledge of the crossing of Jordan and these recent victories at Jericho and Ai, but to completely play their deceptive role, they would not so much as mention these. They represented themselves as coming from a distance and as not having heard of any aggression on western Palestine.

The mortal does not remember the Lord; he wanders around, engrossed in greed. Committing sins, he dies, and his life ends in an instant. His body is like a clay vessel or a brittle metal pot. If you wish to keep it safe and sound, then meditate on the Lord; Chant the Name of the Lord. Chanting His Name night and day, the Lord will eventually hear your call. Says Kabeer : the body is a banana forest, and the mind is an intoxicated elephant. The jewel of spiritual wisdom is the prod, and the rare Saint is the rider. [1376 SGGS]

He commits innumerable robberies, countless acts of adultery, millions of falsehoods and thousands of abuses. He practices infinite number of deceptions and secret deeds, night and day, against his fellow beings.[471 SGGS]

When man tries to, or thinks of fooling others, by being a master-trickster, he, too, shall, someday, become an unsuspecting victim of his own game plan, developed so very painstakingly, by him. He is sure to have a taste of his own bitter medicine/potion.

The English word *vengeance* is a principal translation of several Hebrew words related to the stem *nqm* and of *ekdikeo* (and cognates) in the Septuagint (or earliest Greek Old Testament) and in the New Testament. Behind the Hebrew usage of *nqm* stands a sense of the solidarity and integrity of the community which, having been damaged by an offense, must be restored by some deed of retaliation or punishment. The range of meaning of the motif, however, extends beyond "vengeance" and/or "punishment" to a sense of "deliverance."

Human revenge against an enemy or enemies is demonstrated in a broad range of circumstances in the Old Testament documents (Gen. 4:23-24; Jer. 20:10). Samson's reaction to his enemies (Judg. 15:7) is so described. Vengeance might be punishment directed toward another who has committed adultery with one's wife (Prov. 6:32-34) or toward a whole ethnic group such as the Philistines (1 Sam. 18:25).

As an activity of God on behalf of His people, *nqm* is sometimes best understood as retribution (Judg. 11:36). David was often the recipient of such favor (2 Sam. 4:8; 22:48; Ps. 18:47). The motif occurs in this sense in the prayers of Jeremiah (Jer. 11:20; 15:15; 20:12) and of the psalmist (Pss. 58:10; 79:10; 94:1). Note that *deliverance* is involved in several of these instances. The wrath of God was exhibited toward Babylon (Jer. 51:6, 11, 36; Isa. 47:3; Ezek. 24:7-9). In the song of Moses, such retribution is attributed to God alone (Deut. 32:35, 41, 43). Yet, the wrath of God might be extended toward the people of Israel because of their sin (Lev. 26:25).

Nqm has a sense of eschatological deliverance. This can be combined with an expression of God's wrath against Israel's enemies (Isa. 34:8). The parallel Isaianic phrases "day of vengeance" and "year of my redemption" have the same import (63:4; compare 61:1-3).

Answer evil with goodness; do not fill the mind with anger, thus your body shall not suffer from any disease, and one shall obtain everything. Says Fareed, the bird (human-being) is a guest in this beautiful world-garden. The morning drums are beating, indicating it is, now, time for departure (moment of death). Musk is distributed during the night ; those in deep slumber shall never become the recipients of their share of this Blessed commodity (hence do not harbor any ill-will towards another, during this short span of a 'night', that is this lifetime).[1381 SGGS]

Do not turn around and strike those who strike you with their fists. Kiss their feet, and return to your own home (DO NOT GENERATE A FEELING OF REMORSEFUL REVENGE, as it is harmful for your progress). When there was time to earn name and fame, by performing worthy deeds, one was in love with the world, instead. [1378 SGGS]

Do not harbor evil intentions against others, and by so doing one shall not be troubled. The Name of the Lord, as preached by the True Guru, is the effective mendicant, and not the Tantric-rituals or the Mantra-recitations or the Yogic-postures. Nanak experiences this peace night and day. [386 SGGS]

Results of Sin had immediate results in the couple's relationship; the self-first and self-only attitude displayed toward God affected the way they looked at one another. The mutual trust and intimacy of the one-flesh bond (Gen. 2:24) was ravaged by distrust. This does not suggest that the knowledge of good and evil was sexual awareness. Intercourse was the command and blessing of God prior to the fall (Gen. 1:28). In the absence of mutual trust, complete intimacy implies complete vulnerability (Gen. 3:7).

The couple also felt compelled to hide from God when they heard Him walking in the garden. When loving trust characterized the couple's attitude, they were apparently comfortable in God's presence. After their sin, shame appropriately marked their relationships—both human and divine (Gen. 3:8). The sinners could not remain hidden. God pursued, asking, "where art thou" (Gen. 3:9). This may be a normal question, but some see it as God's sorrowful anticipation of what follows. Sinners finally must speak to God. Adam admitted that God's presence now provoked fear, and human shame provoked hiding (Gen. 3:10). God's next question drew the man's attention away from his plight to his sin (Gen. 3:11). The couple had to face their maker. The man admitted his sin, but only after emphatically reminding God that the woman was instrumental in his partaking. Woman shared equally in the deed, but she quickly blamed the deceiving serpent (Gen. 3:12-13). Along with shame, blame comes quite naturally to humankind. God moved immediately to punish. The serpent was not interviewed because he was not an image-bearer in whom God sought a representation and relationship. The snake's behavior foreshadowed the reversal of created order and mankind's dominion.

Virtue and sin exist in the body together. [126 SGGS]

O kind father, ignore my sins. [12 SGGS]

The sinners act, and perform nefarious acts (misdeeds), and then they weep and wail, when such acts misfire and backfire. Says Nanak: just as the churning stick churns the butter, so does the Judge of Righteousness torture them. Says Nanak : speaking in Righteousness, one's world (home) becomes sanctified.[1425]

Emulate the one who binds in bondage his evil and corrupted gaze. One who does not know the difference between vice and virtue wanders around uselessly, and aimlessly. [1329 SGGS]

Due to ignorance, egotism, and lust for power, sex and wealth, man has sacrificed man, at the altar, of his multifarious cravings. The height of inhumanism was when man did not think twice, before sacrificing fellow-beings, to appease "GOD. NOW, this is an absurd and ridiculous level, to which man stooped. How could GOD, the FATHER & MOTHER, be asking for the sacrifice of one child, to be perpetrated by another. The same feeble argument (Appeasement of God) has been, repeatedly, advanced, regarding man enslaving man, over the centuries, and for retaining extra-judicial control over others' land, life and family-members. Inhuman and undignified behavior was evident when man forced women to marry several husbands, at any given point in time, and when man had a 'Harem' comprising of hundreds of ladies, for the satisfaction of his carnal-instincts. Religious intolerance was at its pinnacle, but the fanatic was considered to be the most pious one. Discrimination, on account of race, gender, color, creed, status, caste, and religion have been the other indelible black spots, on the canvas. All such thoughts, words and deeds, that are detrimental or prejudicial, to the interests of another, are tantamount to being a "SIN". Quite often, a SIN may be an act of omission, rather than that of commission.

O God my God, what miseries and mockeries did I now experience, when obedience to my teachers was proposed to me, as proper in a boy, in order that in this world I might prosper, and excel in tongue-science, which should serve to the "praise of men," and to deceitful riches. Next I was put to school to get learning, in which I (poor wretch) knew not what use there was; and yet, if idle in learning, I was beaten.

When, then, we ask why a crime was done, we believe it not, unless it appear that there might have been some desire of obtaining some of those, which we called lower goods, or a fear of losing them. For they are beautiful and comely; although compared with those higher and beatific goods, they are abject and low. A man hath murdered another; why? He loved his wife or his estate; or would rob for his own livelihood; or feared to lose some such things by him; or, wronged, was on fire to be revenged. Would any commit murder upon no cause, delighted simply in murdering? Who would believe it?

His Friend Being Snatched Away by Death, He Imagines that He Remains Only as Half. But what speak I of these things? For now is no time to question, but to confess unto Thee. Wretched I was; and wretched is every soul bound by the friendship of perishable things; he is torn asunder when he loses them, and then he feels the wretchedness, which he had ere yet he lost them. So was it then with me; I wept most bitterly, and found my repose in bitterness. Thus was I wretched, and that wretched life I held dearer than my friend. For though I would willingly have changed it, yet was I more unwilling to part with it than with him.

It is futile to pin hopes on a human-being (mortal). One must, instead, dwell upon the Giver, the Provider, God, and the Only One.

Reliance on mortals is in vain — know this well. The Great Giver is the One Lord God. By His gifts, we are contented, and we suffer from thirst no longer. The One Lord (Himself, the Creator) destroys, and also preserves and sustains. Human beings exercise no control, whatsoever, over any incident in life. Understanding His Order, there is peace. So take His Name, and wear it as your necklace. Remember God, and meditate. Guarantees NANAK : " NO obstacle shall deter you, during your victorious march, towards self-reliance". [281 SGGS]

The Lord is the Fulfiller of desires, the Giver of total peace; the Kaamadhaynaa (the mythological wish-fulfilling cow), is His slave. So meditate on such a Lord, O my soul. Then, one shall obtain total peace, O mind, Chant the True Name (Sat Naam). In this world, and in the world beyond, such a face shall be radiant, by meditating continually on the Immaculate Lord. [669 SGGS]

Luke 1: 13, 14, 15.
The angel told Zechariah: "God has heard your prayers. Your wife Elizabeth shall have a son, and you must name him John. His birth will make you very happy, and many people will be glad. Your son will be a great servant of the Lord. He must never drink wine or beer, and the power of the Holy Spirit will be with him from the time he is born".

DRUNKENNESS A state of dizziness, headaches, and vomiting resulting from drinking alcoholic beverages. From Genesis 9:21 on, the Bible describes the shameful state of the drunken person and the shameful actions resulting from the state. Too much partying led to drunkenness and failure of communication between husband and wife (1 Sam. 25:36). It left a person defenseless against enemies (1 Kings 16:9-10; 20:16). They sang loud songs ridiculing other people (Ps. 69:12) and could not walk straight (Job 12:25; Ps. 107:27). They vomited (Jer. 25:27) and were in a daze, unaware of events around them (Joel 1:5).

They ruined their future (Prov. 23:20-21). They could not protect themselves against unnecessary injuries such as avoiding a thorn bush (Prov. 26:9). Drunken leaders ruin a nation (Isa. 28:1-9). Being drunk became a figure of speech for having to drink the disaster God was sending (Isa. 49:26; 51:21-22; Jer. 25:27-29; Ezek. 39:17-20.

The Jewish leaders tried to discredit Jesus, saying He was a drunkard (Matt. 11:19). Jesus warned that the cares of life may lead to anxiety and drunkenness (Luke 21:34). Paul repeatedly warned against the dangers of drunkenness (Rom. 13:13; 1 Cor. 5:11; Gal. 5:21; 1 Thess. 5:7). 1 Timothy 3:3 and Titus 1:7 warn church leaders they must not be drunkards. Drunkenness is a pagan custom, not a Christian one (1 Pet. 4:3). Drunkards are among these who will not "inherit the kingdom of God" (1 Cor. 6:10).

Those who consume liquor, err. True inebriation results from God's reminiscence. [399 SGGS]

One person brings a full bottle, and another comes to fill his cup. Drinking it, his intelligence departs, and madness enters his mind. [554 SGGS]

Those who indulge in any kind of intoxicants, such as smoking and drugs etc., and do not contemplate the Lord, — the Messenger of Death will seize them and take them away.[726]

Do not get lost in the GAMBLE (the games of chance, or other self-deceptive sensual-pleasures).[80 SGGS]

Great, thoughtful, wise, learned ones have been known to behave like animals, under the influence of liquor. [328 SGGS].

The Messenger of Death could arrive in the guise of any deadly disease, such as cancer or emphysema. Addiction of any kind is a vice that shall ruin the body and the mind. The ramifications of such deeds shall be far-reaching and horrific, at times. Gambling is another cruel vice that shatters the peace of households, and results in penury and hunger. One fails to comprehend the distinction between right and wrong, between life and death, and between Sin and Virtue. When one is under these influences it is impossible to draw the line of demarcation. NOW, the DEVIL is in 'Total-Command', thereby awarding a Free-Reign to the addictive substances, who indulge in their passionate-play, designed to wreaking havoc, and reducing the consumer to a physical and mental wreck. On a different and more significant plane, of Morality, one loses the power to differentiate between 'Love & Lust', between one's own spouse, and that of another. Under the demonic influences, one cannot realize whether one is acting sinfully and disgracefully, with one's daughter, sister or mother, succumbing to the temptation of sexual indulgence and promiscuity. Incest, no longer, remains an improbability, and that is the most horrendous of all known SINS.

I tell you not to worry about your life. Don't worry about having
something to eat or wear. Life is more than food or clothing. Look at
the crows. They don't plant or harvest, and they don't have
storehouses or barns. But God takes care of them. Can worry make
you live longer? Luke 12: 22, 23, 24, 25.

"We were hoping that it was He who was going to redeem Israel.
Indeed, besides all this, today is the third day since these things
happened" (Luke 24:21).

Every fact that the disciples stated was right, but the conclusions they
drew from those facts were wrong. Anything that has even a hint of
dejection spiritually is always wrong. If I am depressed or burdened, I
am to blame, not God or anyone else. Dejection stems from one of two
sources—I have either satisfied a lust or I have not had it satisfied. In
either case, dejection is the result. What have I been hoping or trusting
God would do? Is today "the third day" and He has still not done what
I expected? Am I therefore justified in being dejected and in blaming
God? Whenever we insist that God should give us an answer to prayer
we are off track. The purpose of prayer is that we get a hold of God,
not of the answer. It is impossible to be well physically and to be
dejected, because dejection is a sign of sickness. This is also true
spiritually. Dejection spiritually is wrong, and we are always to blame
for it.

Anxiety may range from genuine concern (see Phil. 2:20, 28; 2 Cor.
11:28) to obsessions that originate from a distorted perspective of life
(Matt. 6:25-34; Mark 4:19; Luke 12:22-31). Jesus did not prohibit
genuine concern about food or shelter, but He did teach that we should
keep things in their proper perspective. We should make God's
kingdom our first priority; everything else will fall in line after we do
that (Matt. 6:33).

The fickle consciousness does not remain stable. Enshrining the Lord's lotus feet in one's consciousness, one lives long. Everyone else has worries and anxieties. [932 SGGS]

Everyone appears to be worried; by meditating upon the One True Lord does a worried person get relief from anxiety. In one's heart having the Lord's Noumenon, one enjoys bliss, and is liberated, receiving honor in His Court [991 SGGS].

The mind is filled to the brim, with bliss, since the time of hearing about God's arrival. All sorrows have departed, and body, mind and soul are all rejuvenated. Prays Nanak : "when I met the Lord of excellence, I came to experience all pleasure and bliss".[459 SGGS]

The ramifications arising out of extreme worry are really serious. An extremely worried and tormented person could commit suicide, or could go insane. Worry is such a raging fire that destroys the mental-equilibrium and the physical-capabilities. Worry pertains to past events, having possible repercussions, in the future. And, NOT living in the present is a serious 'disease'. But, this style and art of living cannot be mastered without serious inclination, tempered with meditation. Multitudes continue to grope in the dark corridors, of imaginary hallucinations. Furthermore, superstition and 'fear of the unknown' have an additional deleterious effect on the faculties of the mind. NOW, all of this seems and sounds to be (and rather, it, actually, is) really absurd, considering the time-tested fact that man exercises, absolutely, NO control over results. Otherwise, if man had control over situations and results, or could rectify/remedy a situation, by worrying, nothing would ever go wrong, after one would implement a particular plan-of-action. ULTIMATE CELESTIAL BLISS can be attained, only, by living in the present. Pious thinking and Meditation upon God's Name are intertwined. Meditation and prayer could be performed in solitary confinement, or even in Congregations. Attending spiritual-discourses and sermons, delivered by the pious whose vision and verbosity is capable of relieving the worried mind, and of providing it with the much-needed solace and stability.

Natural Evil Concerning natural evil, several emphases should be noted. First, moral evil accounts for much of natural evil. In Genesis, evil and suffering appeared only after the Fall (Gen. 3:16-19). By contrast, the original creation is very good (Gen. 1:31). The new heavens and new earth will have no more suffering (Rev. 21:4). This means that evil and suffering are not eternally inevitable. Rather they are bound up with the actions of sinful humans and angelic beings. Physical suffering and pain and finally death have been introduced as a consequence of the Fall (Gen. 3:16-19).

Second, God disciplines His people collectively and individually, even through natural evil and pain, to bring them closer to His purposes (Prov. 3:11-12; Jer. 18:1-10). This emphasis is also found in the New Testament (Heb. 2:10; 5:8-9; 12:5-11).

Third, personal life cannot develop except in a stable environment. God limited Himself by the establishment of regularity and law. This regularity of nature is an important factor in developing human personality. The earthquake, volcano, and storm, which cause human suffering, all belong to nature's regularity. Some so-called natural evil, therefore, can be attributed to the necessary operation of natural uniformities.

Fourth, natural evils may be used for judgment upon sin. It is deeply ingrained in the Bible that physical evils have been used by God for the punishment of individual and national wickedness. Noah's flood, the destruction of Sodom and Gomorrah, and the fall of Jerusalem are examples. This does not mean that all physical evils are the punishment of physical sins.

Moral Evil There are many biblical teachings which help us to understand moral evil from the Christian perspective.

God, the world is burning in its own sins. Save it through your mercy.
[853 SGGS]

The 'demonic Evil' manifests itself in negative thoughts, harsh words, and cruel deeds, perpetrated against another, consequently bringing great suffering for both (oppressor and oppressed) in the long run.

The pain of separation is as unbearable as the pain of extreme hunger. The greatest, and unendurable, pain is the attack of the Messenger of Death. Another pain is the disease consuming my body. O doctor, don't administer the medicine. The pain persists, and the body continues to suffer. This medicine has no effect. Forgetting his Lord and Master, the mortal enjoys sensual pleasures; then, disease wells up in his body. The blind (ignorant/foolish) mortal receives his punishment. The value of sandalwood lies in its fragrance. The value of a human lasts only as long as the breath in the body. When the breath is taken away, the body crumbles into dust. The mortal's body emanates a golden-aura, and the soul-swan is immaculate and pure, if even a tiny particle of the Immaculate Name resides within. Only then shall all pain and disease be eradicated. Says Nanak:"the mortal is saved through the True Name".[1256 SGGS]

Worldly possessions are obtained by pain and suffering; when they are gone, they leave pain and suffering. Says Nanak : without the True Name, hunger is never satisfied. Beauty does not satisfy hunger; when the man sees beauty, he hungers even more. As many as are the pleasures of the body, so many are
the pains, which afflict it.[1287 SGGS]

Peter Slept (Acts 12:6) : Peter had no reason, though in prison, to feel that God had forsaken him. The true servant of God can rest in peace even though seemingly in the power of enemies. God is in control to defeat every power that overtakes us. In every place and in all circumstances we are in the hands of Him who is able to deliver us and give us victory over all enemies. Had Peter been inclined to stay awake and bemoan the fact of guards, iron chains and unyielding gates, he would not have been alert to the directions of the angel to lead him out to a place of freedom and beyond the reach of his enemies. Obstacles so often blind our vision. We lose a sense of direction and miss all that God has for us. *"He who is in you is greater than he who is in the world."* (1 John 4:4). Let us rest assured that God is able to keep us in days of trial and tribulation.

Abraham's faith had stood all former tests. It had been strong enough to break the ties that bound him to country, home and kindred. It had endured the many and long delays in the fulfilling of the promises. It had risen above all the obstacles, physical and moral, that stood in the way of the accomplishment of these promises. It had given up Ishmael and accepted Isaac. Would it stand the last demand to give up to God the best-loved thing on earth and to do what appeared to be alien to God's character and contrary to His word and promise? It seemed the command and the promise were in conflict. If he obeyed the command, he frustrated the promise.

God further promised Moses that all obstacles would be removed and the children of Israel would serve God at the very mount where he was given the commission. The "I" of Moses was met with the "I" of God. If God be for us, who can be against us? Little did Moses realize what this promise would mean to him in the future.

Millions of obstacles (innumerable problems) infest and afflict such a person, who forgets (rather, does NOT WANT TO remember) to meditate on God's Name and Grace.   A state of ingratitude, thanklessness and shame. Such a one shall live and die in pain and misery, like a crow trapped in a barren isolated house. [522 SGGS]

The TRUE GURU (Teacher, Guide, Philosopher) would help a serious and worthy disciple, who is spiritually inclined, to master the techniques required for remembering God, under all circumstances. In adversity, it is the natural tendency of human-beings, to pray, for help. But, one who retains the essence of the Lord's Sacred Name, in his soul, even in the season of prosperity, is the Redeemed one. And this would have the somber effect of destroying all obstacles and pain, miseries and tormentations, in the life of the devotee.[622 SGGS]

Misery is a medicinal remedy, and affluence is a disease, so say the Sikh Gurus.   During enjoyments, one fails to remember God, the provider of all luxury, while in pain and poverty, one falls back upon Him, as the 'last refuge', for support and solace. All obstacles should be looked upon as great challenges for one's growth, mentally and spiritually. Many significant lessons are to be learnt, which would serve one in good stead. Instead of always complaining about lack of something in one's life, or instead of laying the blame for one's failure and misery on another person's doorstep, one must find try to decode the 'secret messages' in the obstacles.   Hurdles lead to eventual progress.   Someone who never rode a horse, and someone who has never fallen from it, time and again, would never learn how to become a master jockey, who would later go on to control the most stubborn of the equine species. Even, the birds must overcome resistance and yet they succeed in flying high.

If one member only be corrupt, and we do not cut it off, it will carry the whole body to hell, Matt. 5:29, 30. Saul was commanded to slay all God's enemies, the Amalekites; and he slew all but Agag, and the saving him alive proved his ruin. Caleb and Joshua entered into God's promised rest, because they wholly followed the Lord, Numb. 14:24, and 32:11, 12, Deut. 1:36. Josh. 14:6, 8, 9, 14. Naaman's hypocrisy appeared in that, however ever he seemed to be greatly affected with gratitude to God for healing his leprosy, and engaged to serve him, yet in one thing he desired to be excused.

So the Scripture never uses such emphatic expressions concerning any other signs of hypocrisy, and unsoundness of heart, as concerning an unholy practice. So Gal. 6:7, "Be not deceived; God is not mocked; for whatsoever a man soweth, that shall he also reap." 1 Cor. 6:9, 10, "Be not deceived; neither fornicators, nor idolaters, &c., shall inherit the kingdom of God."

And for us to make that great which the Scripture makes little, and that little which the Scripture makes great, tends to give us a monstrous idea of religion; and (at least indirectly and gradually) to lead us wholly away from the right rule, and from a right opinion of ourselves, and to establish delusion and hypocrisy. Nor is there much encouragement, in the experience of present or past times, to lay down rules or marks to distinguish between true and false affections, in hopes of convincing any considerable number of that sort of hypocrites, who have been deceived with great false discoveries and affections, and are once settled in a false confidence, and high conceit of their own supposed great experiences and privileges. Such hypocrites are so conceited of their own wisdom, and so blinded and hardened with a very great self-righteousness (but very subtle and secret, under the disguise of great humility).

The herons in their white feathers dwell in the sacred shrines of pilgrimage. They tear apart and eat the living beings, and so they are not called white. This body is like the simmal tree; people are fooled on seeing it. Its fruits are useless — just like the qualities of this body. The blind man is carrying such a heavy load, and his journey through the mountains is so long and treacherous. These eyes can see, but cannot find the Way. How does one climb up and cross over the mountain? What good does it do to serve, and be good, and be clever? Says Nanak : contemplate the Name of the Lord, and one shall be released from bondage. [729 SGGS]

"Oh deceived Mind! Why did you not adhere to the teachings of the learned and accomplished GURU? What good is it   shaving off the head, and donning an orange-colored attire (garb/guise) with the intention of conning people, into believing you as a pious soul. Is it a worthy and justifiable deed, to be masquerading in a disguise? Bidding adieu to Truth, this life shall be wasted, under the influence of Falsehood. All deeds, so far, have been to eat, sleep, and make merry, in gay- abandon, like a carefree-animal (instincts are identical to those of animals). Remember that this form of life is lived at a baser-level, and not when one is granted the Great Human-Birth. [633 SGGS]

One's hypocrisy shall be exposed, sooner or later. Therefore, one is advised to pay heed, and listen to the beneficial advice of the Lord Master, and take pre-emptive action, before falling deep into the darkest dungeons of death. Realization of one's judgmental-errors and fallibilities and fallacies, should dawn while one is alive. Only then is there any chance of being rescued.

LUST In contemporary usage, a strong craving or desire, especially sexual desire. KJV and earlier English versions frequently used lust in the neutral sense of desire. This older English usage corresponded to the use of the underlying Hebrew and Greek terms which could be used in a positive sense: of the desire of the righteous (Prov. 10:24), of Christ's desire to eat the Passover with His disciples (Luke 22:15), or of Paul's desire to be with Christ (Phil. 1:23). Since lust has taken on the primary meaning of sexual desire, modern translations often replace the KJV's lust with a term with a different nuance. NRSV, for example, used crave/craving (Num. 11:34; Ps. 78:18); covet (Rom. 7:7); desire (Ex. 15:9; Prov. 6:25; 1 Cor. 10:6); long for (Rev. 18:14).

The unregenerate (preconversion) life is governed by deceitful lusts or desires (Eph. 4:22; 2:3; Col. 3:5; Tit. 2:12). Following conversion, such fleshly desires compete for control of the individual with spiritual desires (Gal. 5:16-17; 2 Tim. 2:22). First John 2:16-17 warns that desires of the flesh and eyes are not from God and will pass away with the sinful world. Here lust or desire includes not only sexual desire but also other vices such as materialism. James 1:14-15 warns that desire is the beginning of all sin and results in death. Jesus warned that one who lusts, has already sinned (Matt. 5:28). Part of God's judgment on sin is to give persons over to their own desires (Rom. 1:24). Only the presence of the Holy Spirit in the life of the believer makes victory over sinful desires possible (Rom. 8:1-2).

Beauty and sexual desire are friends; hunger and tasty food are tied together. Greed is bound up in its search for wealth, and sleep will use even a tiny space as a bed. Anger barks and brings ruin on itself, blindly pursuing useless conflicts. It is good to be silent, because without the Name of the Lord, one's mouth spews forth only filth. Royal power, wealth, beauty, social status and youth are the five thieves. These thieves have plundered the world; no one's honor has been spared. But these thieves themselves are robbed, by those who fall at the Guru's Feet.[1288 SGGS]

Overflowing with sexual desire, one's intellect is stained with darkness; In the heat of youthful passion, one looks with desire upon the faces of other men's wives, unable to distinguish between good and evil. Drunk with sexual desire and other great sins, one goes astray, and does not distinguish between vice and virtue.[93 SGGS]

O Lord and Master, in ignorance this mind is sold out, and is, now, in Illusion's hands. Lord and Master, the Guru of the World, here's a lustful being of the Dark Iron-Age (KaliYuga). The five vices have corrupted the mind. Moment by moment, they lead the mind further away from the Lord. [710 SGGS]

Others' spouses, others' wealth, greed, egotism, corruption, evil passions, slander of others, sexual desire and anger — all of these are like venom; give up all these.[1255 SGGS]

Lustful indulgence or promiscuity and anger bring the human body to ruin and misery, thereby reducing it's value from gold to dust / ashes (twasting a golden opportunity made available for remembering God and serving others). [932 SGGS]

Unbridled behavior is the sole cause of the spread of the deadly epidemic called AIDS, along with several other life-endangering diseases.

Mortals can commit blunders, under the influence of anger, but God's anger is portrayed hereunder.

While Israel abode in Shittim the people commit whoredom with the daughters of Moab, v. 1. They become idolaters, v. 2. The anger of the Lord is kindled against them, and he commands the ringleaders to be hanged, vv. 3, 4. Moses causes the judges to slay the transgressors, v. 5. Zimri, one of the Israelitish princes of the tribe of Simeon, brings a Midianitish princess, named Cozbi, into his tent, while the people are deploring their iniquity before the tabernacle, v. 6.

Reuben went and lay with Bilhah his father's concubine— Jonathan, in his Targum, says that Reuben only overthrew the bed of Bilhah, which was set up opposite to the bed of his mother Leah, and that this was reputed to him as if he had lain with her. The colouring given to the passage by the Targumist is, that Reuben was incensed, because he found Bilhah preferred after the death of Rachel to his own mother Leah; and therefore in his anger he overthrew her couch. The same sentiment is repeated by Jonathan, and glanced at by the Jerusalem Targum, Genesis 49:4. Could this view of the subject be proved to be correct, both piety and candor would rejoice.

In the morrow all the congregation—murmured—It is very likely that the people persuaded themselves that Moses and Aaron had used some cunning in this business, and that the earthquake and fire were artificial; else, had they discerned the hand of God in this punishment, could they have dared the anger of the Lord in the very face of justice? **Cursed David by his gods—**Prayed his gods to curse him. This long parley between David and Goliath is quite in the style of those times. A Hindu sometimes in a fit of anger says to his enemy, The goddess Kali shall devour thee! May Durga destroy thee! Homer's heroes have generally an altercation before they engage.

169

Sheikh Fareed advises: answer evil with goodness; do not fill your mind with anger. Then this body shall not suffer from any disease, and one shall obtain everything. [1381 SGGS]

One who has an abiding faith in the Holy-Word, God resides within him (body and soul). He does not come or go in reincarnation, and he is rescued. Through the Word of the Guru, his heart-lotus blossoms forth. Whoever is seen, is driven by hope and despair, by sexual desire, anger, corruption, hunger and thirst. Says Nanak: those detached recluses who meet the Lord are so very rare.[224 SGGS]

Sexual desire and anger are very powerful in the body; bless this devotee with courage and fortitude that he may rise to wage war against them, and that he may emerge victorious. Lord, please treat me as Your Own and save ; through the Perfect Guru, drive them out. The powerful fire of corruption is raging violently within; the Word of the Immaculate Guru is the icy-water, which soothes the body, and provides solace to the mind. The mind and body are calm and tranquil; the disease has been cured, and now there's peaceful sleep. As the rays of the sun spread out everywhere, the Lord pervades each and every heart. Meeting the Holy Saint, one drinks in the Sublime Essence of the Lord; sitting in the home of the inner being, drink in the essence of His Name.[1325 SGGS]

Anger could be the consequence of an array of feelings and emotions, including victimization and betrayal, powerlessness, insecurity, failure in communication, and a host of related causes. To keep the demonic-force of Anger, at bay, one could deploy the technique of ' stepping-back ', or even think in terms of adopting a novel-method of self-imposition of a penal-action, for each defeat at the hands of Anger.

New Testament Teaching By the time the New Testament books were written, God had led their authors to a clear-cut doctrine of Satan. This doctrine located an origin of evil in Satan. This recognizes the reality of evil outside and beyond the scope of human will. The New Testament avoids identifying evil with the direct will of God and keeps it always and finally subordinate to God.

Matthew, Mark, and Luke clearly accept and teach a doctrine of a personal Satan and his agents called fallen angels or demons (Mark 3:22). Matthew 4:1 tells of Jesus being tempted by the devil in the wilderness. In Matthew 25:41 even hell is described as being prepared for the devil and his angels. Satan and demons are seen as able to inflict disease (Matt. 17:5-18; Luke 13:16). Satan possessed Judas (Luke 22:3). John saw Satan as the prince of this world (John 12:31; 14:30; 16:11) with the whole world in his power (1 John 5:19).

The apostle Paul's worldview teaches that Satan is the god of this age. The cosmos or unredeemed world is at present under Satan's power. Satan is now the "commander of the spiritual powers of the air" (Eph. 2:2 REB) and leads "the superhuman forces of evil in the heavenly realms" (Eph. 6:12 REB).

The general New Testament Epistles describe Satan's activities graphically. Second Peter 2:4 speaks of the "angels that sinned" and Jude 6 of the "angels, which kept not their first estate." The constant use of violence and deceit by Satan requires that believers manifest courage and extreme vigilance (Jas. 4:7; 1 Pet. 5:8-9).

The book of Revelation sees Satan's activities as involving not only individuals but also communities. Political forces can become servants of the devil (Rev. 12; 13). Revelation 2:13 even speaks of a throne of Satan.

They may live in heavenly realms, and conquer the nine regions of the world, but if they forget the Lord of the world, they are just wanderers in the wilderness. In the midst of millions of games and entertainment, the Lord's Name does not come to reside in their minds and hearts. Their home is like a wilderness, in the depths of hell. He sees the terrible, awful wilderness as a city. Gazing upon the false objects, he believes them to be real. Engrossed in sexual desire, anger and egotism, he wanders around insane. When the Messenger of Death hits him on the head with his club, then he regrets and repents. Without the Perfect, Divine Guru, he roams around like Satan.[707 SGGS]

Cruelty is the handiwork of devilish tendencies, which have resulted in massive spillage of blood on the face of the earth. The Gurus say that there is no such entity as a devil, all the negative vices have been considered to be the manifestations of the devil.

Christianity & Sikhism
Commonalities & Differences : A Synopsis

The Origins:
Both, Christianity and Sikhism started as per Divine Will.
Christianity developed, as Command to Jesus Christ.
Sikhism sprang up as a Revelation to Guru Nanak.
Each established a firm and distinct identity. From another standpoint, both claim to be revolutionary protest movements, launched to bring about a radical transformation in the psyche of the masses; both rebelled against ritualism, superstitious beliefs, prejudices, and ceremonial legacies.

The Founders:
As per Christian belief, Jesus Christ was sent by God to liberate sinners, and he proclaimed himself as 'Son of God'.

As per Sikh belief, Guru Nanak was anointed through Divine Revelation, and he proclaimed himself as 'Servant of God', though he has been described by his contemporaries as God-incarnate.

Divine Light:
Jesus had several disciples, but no successor to, physically, embody the Divine Light.

The Divine Light, originating in Guru Nanak was transmitted to nine successive Gurus, in human-form, before finally being preserved, for eternity, in the Holy Scripture, Guru Granth Sahib.

Birth of the Founders:
Both were born, "not as a will of the flesh, but of God".
Jesus Christ was born as a result of a virginal conception, as per Divine Will.
Guru Nanak, while enjoying Divine Fellowship, was assigned to the temporal world, not as a result of the 'Karmic' principle of reincarnation.

Scriptures:

The 66 books of the present-day Bible were written by about 40 writers, over a period of two centuries; No original writing of Christ is available.

In Sikhism, the Original works, authored by Guru Nanak, his successors and other Saints are included in the SGGS. This scripture is written and compiled by the Gurus, themselves, in their lifetime.

Baptism/Initiation :

Both religions have special, specific, elaborate and formal ceremonies.

During the First Baptism, in Christianity, Jesus Christ requests John, a disciple, to baptize him.

In Sikhism, Guru Gobind Singh, the Tenth Master of the House of Guru Nanak (Founder of Sikh Faith) pleads with his five disciples to initiate him, into the 'Order-of-the-Khalsa'.

Creation of the Universe:

Both subscribe to the view that there are countless galaxies, and constellations; man cannot gauge God's extent and expansiveness, He is beyond time, space, and human comprehension; unfathomable.

Christianity believes that God created a heaven and earth, and then for six days God added rivers and mountains, various species and vegetation etc., before finally resting, on the 7th day (Sunday).

Sikhism believes that God created the entire Universe with a single command; all at once, not in phases.

Idol-Worship:

Both, Christianity and Sikhism do not believe in it; Sikh Gurus did not seek to be venerated. Instead, the Scriptural Writings are given paramountcy. Both religions disfavor idolatry (statues, symbols, icons, photographs).

Status of the Holy Congregation:
In Christianity, it is called a 'flock of sheep'.

In Sikhism, it is designated at 'par with the Guru'.

Status of woman:
Christianity believes that God created woman from the rib of Adam, and named her Eve. The Scripture also says that a woman shall be condemned to live under the domination of man.

Sikhism believes that both, woman and man enjoy equal status.

Power of Prayer:
Both believe in it. Holy Congregation's Prayers assume Powers of healing. These prayers are heard in the Lord's Court, and suffering humanity is rescued, as per God's Word enshrined in the Holy Books.
Both believe that where there are two or more adherents, in collective prayer, there resides God.

Meditation:
Forgetting the Lord is virtual 'death'. Paul says: "I die daily" (suffering separation from God).

This is similar to Sikh thought, "I live by remembering Him, I die when I forget Him".

Sin:
The Scriptures of Christianity say that Adam's disobedience made the world population sinners, forever. And, so death passed upon all men, for that all have sinned.

Sikhism does not believe that procreation is a sin; it is very much in consonance with God's Own design.

Salvation:
Christian belief advocates that all who believe in Christ shall enjoy heavenly realms, on being sanctified. Some denominations believe that all people are born sinners, and that they must have faith in the Only Begotten Son of God, to be saved.

175

Scripture of Sikhism belives that all are born blessed, and human birth is given as a golden chance to realize God. One could be granted Salvation, even if one does not subscribe to the views and preaching of Sikhism.

Atonement/Repentance:
Christianity believes Christ atoned for all sinners. It lays emphasis on repentance, rather than righteousness. One repentant sinner is considered to be better than a million righteous, pious Christians.

Sikhism believes "the hand that sins, suffers the punishment; all are accountable, individually". It stresses upon both, righteousness as well as repentance, in that order.

Reincarnation:
Christian belief is that there is no reincarnation: the body of a believer shall enjoy heavenly abode, once Jesus resurrects that blessed one from the grave, on the Day of Redemption/Judgment.

Sikhism believes that a liberated Soul shall enjoy everlasting Communion with God, while a condemned sinner shall continue to migrate in 8.4 million reincarnations.

Heaven & Hell :
Christianity believes that all who believe in Christ shall go to heaven, while non-believers shall rot in hell; firm faith in a physical heaven and hell.

Sikhism believes that all who become the recipients of God's Grace, through pious living, shall be redeemed, here on earth, in this lifetime, and those who do not qualify, due to their sinful misdemeanor, shall experience hell, here on earth, in various forms. Heaven exists where God is remembered, and is not another realm. No belief in a physical realm of heaven or hell.

Angels & Devils:
Christianity believes there are Guardian Angels for each true believer, and Devil, for the non-believer.

Sikhism believes those who live a virtuous life are Angels, and those committing sins are devils.

Missionary System:
Christianity has a hierarchical missionary system. A priest can pardon or redeem a sinner, who 'confesses'.

Sikhism does not have a specific pyramidical set-up. A priest cannot pardon or redeem a sinner. Only God has the power to pardon, directly, without a mediator.

Ascetism:
In Christianity, ascetism and celibacy is encouraged, as ways and means of serving humanity.

In Sikhism, the life of a householder is encouraged, as a potent vehicle for serving humanity. Also, it is considered a natural way of life, because the 'attraction' for it is unavoidable, even though a person remains a celibate; hence, the desired fruits of celibacy are not reaped.

God is Spirit:
Christianity believes God is Trinitarian: God is the Father, the Son, and the Holy Spirit, all simultaneously, and yet He is not three Gods but only One God.

Sikhism believes in the existence of Only One God, whose Spirit is manifest in the form of all living organisms.

God's manifestation as 'Divine Command':
Both emphasize upon the reality of God as 'The Word' as revealed through the Prophets.

The Supreme Power
Both believe the infiniteness of God; He is eternal, with no beginning and no end; He is in full control of all Creation.

Is God 'Partisan' ?
Bible says God has favorite people, chosen countries and tribes. God punishes those he doesn't like, and, while exercising His discretionary

powers, may pardon and also reward sinners, if they happen to be His chosen ones.

Sikhism believes God loves all humanity, as His very own; all are equals.

Is God 'Jealous' ?
Christianity believes that He is jealous (He sought vengeance against those who did not pay heed to His Command; He sent invaders, caused epidemics and floods, as a measure of his anger, to punish those opposing his favourites).

Sikhism discounts that God is jealous; He does not seek vengeance.

God's repentance:
Christianity believes God repented having created man and other creations, and it grieved Him at His heart.

Sikhism believes: "Creator is perfect, infallible; creations are fallible"

Love for, and Service to humanity:
Both are vociferous in the condemnation of religious fanaticism, and conversions by deployment of force, or persuasion; it is all right if one were to embrace a religion of one's own volition, totally voluntarily. Both believe in the dictum : "Service to humanity is service to GOD"; upliftment of weaker sections of society. Both encourage the practice of 'tithe' (donating ten per cent of one's honest earnings to charity).

Addictions:
Both preach that all addictions/vices (adultery, prostitution, gambling, drugs, etc.) result in Sin, Suffering, and Evil.

Bibliography

Holy Bible, Contemporary English Version, 1995.
  American Bible Society, New York.

The Founder of Christianity; C. H. Dodd; 1970; Collins, London,
  And Macmillan, New York

Oxford Dictionary of the Christian Church: F. L. Cross and E. A.
  L ivingstone; 2nd edn. 1974; Oxford Univ. Press, London and NY

World Christian Encyclopedia : A Comparative Study of Churches &
  Religions in the Modern World (A.D. 1900-2000); Oxford Univ.
  Press, Nairobi; 1982.

Quick Verse Bible Study Version 6 : Parsons Technology, Hiawatha,
  Iowa.

Dictionary of the Bible : F. C. Grant and H. H. Rowley; 2nd edn. 1963.

Cambridge History of The Bible : various Authors & Editors;
  Cambridge Univ. Press, 1963-70.

The Book of Mormon; first edn. 1830; current 1981: published by The
  Church of Jesus Christ of Latter-Day Saints, Salt Lake City,
  Utah, U. S. A.

The Phenomenon of Christianity; N. Smart; Collins, London, 1979.

Light From Light: An Anthology of Christian Mysticism; L. Dupre
  and J. Wiseman; 1988, Paulist Press, New York.

Sikhism & Christianity : W. Owen Cole & Sardar Piara Singh Sambhi
  Macmillan 1993.

Concise Dictionary of Religions.
  Livingstone; Oxford Univ. Press, 2nd Edition 1974.

Sikhism & Christianity : Sardar G. S. Sidhu

The Penguin Dictionary of Religions: J. R. Hinnels (Editor); 1984
  London.

Religions in the Modern World (A.D. 1900-2000); D. B. Barrett;
  Oxford 1982.

Witness to the World : The Christian Mission in Theological
Perspective; 1980; D. J. Bosch; Marshall, Morgan and Scott, London.

The Gospel According to St. John: C. K. Barrett; 1975, S.P.C.K.

God was in Christ: D. M. Balillie; 1947, Faber.

Holy Shri Guru Granth Sahib.

Dictionary of Guru Granth Sahib: Surindar Singh Kohli,
      first edn. 1996; Singh Brothers publishers, Amritsar.

Gurbani CD : Singh Sahib Sant Singh Khalsa (M.D.)
      S. Kulbir Singh & S. Jaswant Singh

Sikhism: S Comparative Study of Its Theology and Mysticism:
      Daljeet Singh; Singh Brothers, Amritsar; India.1994.

Guru Granth Sahib: Interpretations, Meaning and Nature;
      Gurnek Singh; 1998; National Book Shop, Delhi, India.

The Sikh Diaspora: N. G. Barrier and V. A. Dusenbury; 1991,
      Manohar publishers, New Delhi, India.

The Concept of Man; Lajwanti Lahori; published by Munshiram
      Manoharlal, New Delhi; India, 1985.

Trinity of Sikhism : Pritam Singh Gill; 1973; New Academic
      Publishing Co., Jullunder, Punjab, India.

The Sikhs of Punjab; J. S. Grewal; Cambridge Univ. Press; 1994.

The Sikh Faith : Dr. Gurbaksh Singh; 1997; SGPC, Amritsar, India.

The Sikhs, Their Religious Beliefs & Practices : W. Oven Cole &
      Sardar Piara Singh Sambhi; Routledge 1978; 3rd rep. 1989.

The Sikh Religion : M. A. Macauliffe; Oxford Delhi.
      1909; rep. 1963 & 1978

The Singh Sabha and Other Socio-Religious Movements in the
      Punjab: Ganda Singh (Editor); Punjabi University, 2nd edn. 1984.

Sikhism: its Ideals and Institutions: Teja Singh; Orient Longman,
      1938, rep. 1964.

Hum Hindu Nahin: Kahn Singh Nabha; 1984 translated by Jarnail
      Singh; The Sikh Social and Educational Society, Willowdale,
      Canada.

A History Of The Sikhs: Khushwant Singh; 1963 London, Princeton,
      and 1977 Oxford Univ. Press, New Delhi, India.

The Doctrine of Ultimate Reality in Sikh Religion: J. Massey; 1992,
      Manohar Publishers, New Delhi.

Author, Harsimran Singh, Ph.D., and his wife
Satnam Kaur, M.D., presenting a manuscript of
<u>*The Spiritual Power,*</u>
the first book of its kind on
Spirituality in Christianity
to
First Lady Mrs. Hillary Rodham Clinton.